I0606240

PRAISE FOR

THE SEISMIC SHIFT IN YOU

"We've got good leadership all wrong. Effective leaders are not cold, transactional, or manipulative. They're real. Present. Authentic. Connected. *The Seismic Shift in You* shatters the outdated model and shows you exactly what kind of leaders get results—and why it matters. Drs. Michelle Johnston and Marshall Goldsmith nailed it. This book is the shift we need."

MEL ROBBINS, *New York Times* bestselling author and host of *The Mel Robbins Podcast*

"*The Seismic Shift in You* is a profoundly important book for leaders who understand that true connection begins from within. Michelle Johnston and Marshall Goldsmith expertly guide readers through actionable, meaningful shifts that transform not just how we lead but how we show up in every area of our lives. Their emphasis on genuine human connection, vulnerability, and the intentional energy we bring to our interactions resonates deeply with my own leadership philosophy, where people matter first and foremost. This book is not just insightful; it's essential reading for anyone committed to becoming a more effective, authentic, and connected leader. Highly recommended!"

GARRY RIDGE, Chairman Emeritus, WD-40 Company and The Culture Coach; bestselling author of *Any Dumb-Ass Can Do It*

"In a world that demands more from leaders than ever before, *The Seismic Shift in You* delivers a timely blueprint for what it truly means to lead with a lens of connection. This book doesn't just talk about leadership—it challenges you to rewire how you show up for others and for yourself. It's bold, honest, and deeply human. If you're ready to go beyond performance and step into real influence, this is your guide."

ERICA DHAWAN, bestselling author of *Digital Body Language*

"In *The Seismic Shift in You,* Michelle Johnston and Marshall Goldsmith deliver a master class in modern leadership. With heart, clarity, and hard-won wisdom, they show that true transformation doesn't come from more goals or grit—it comes from real human connection. This book is a wake-up call and a road map for any leader ready to evolve from competent to truly compelling. It's not just a shift in strategy—it's a shift in soul."

LAURA GASSNER OTTING, *Wall Street Journal* bestselling author of *Wonderhell*

"Every once in a while, we have the privilege of reading a book that's 'the whole package.' Real-life stories. Thought-provoking insights. Actionable next steps. This book has them all. Read it and reap."

SAM HORN, founder and CEO of The Intrigue Agency and author of *Talking on Eggshells: Soft Skills for Hard Conversations*

"This book is all about the shifts you need to make to be a transformational leader. It's your key to show up as the leader you always wanted to be and elevate everyone around you."

ALISA COHN, executive coach and author of *From Start-Up to Grown-Up*

"Before you can shift others, you have to know how to shift yourself. This is the book that shows you how."

MICHAEL BUNGAY STANIER, bestselling author of *The Coaching Habit*

"In *The Seismic Shift in You*, you'll find the kind of leadership wisdom that transforms not just teams, but lives. It beautifully reflects the principles I've believed in throughout my career—clear purpose, people first, and the power of working together. This book reinforces what I've seen time and again: When leaders operate with humility, accountability, and a genuine desire to 'love them up,' performance follows. If you want to lead with connection and build a culture where people bring their best every day, this book will show you the way."

ALAN MULALLY, former CEO of Boeing Commercial Airplanes and Ford Motor Company

"In *The Seismic Shift in You,* Michelle Johnston and Marshall Goldsmith bring heart and humanity to the center of leadership. With deep empathy and wisdom, they reveal a truth too many leaders avoid: Real connection isn't optional—it's everything, including essential to communicating with both clarity and impact. While intellectually leaders may 'know' this, the book is a call to action to 'do' what it takes to connect. Shed the mask of invulnerability, step into authenticity, and lead with purpose. If you want to thrive and bring others along with you, this is your wake-up call. Read it, reflect, and most of all, live it."

MOLLY TSCHANG, founder and CEO of Abella Consulting and Say It Skillfully®

"In an era defined by disconnection and digital overwhelm, this book offers a vital road map for leaders ready to evolve. Grounded in research and enriched by real-world stories, it makes a highly compelling case that leadership in the modern world isn't just about strategy—it's about self-awareness, emotional intelligence, and meaningful human connection."

STEVEN ROGELBERG, PhD, author of *The Surprising Science of Meetings*

"*The Seismic Shift in You* is the rare leadership book that doesn't just offer tools—it invites transformation. Michelle Johnston and Marshall Goldsmith deliver a compelling case for connection as the engine of leadership, and show you how to do it."

DORIE CLARK, executive education faculty at Columbia Business School and *Wall Street Journal* bestselling author of *The Long Game*

"Michelle Johnston and Marshall Goldsmith have created something extraordinary: a book that doesn't just teach leadership principles, but transforms how leaders show up in the world. *The Seismic Shift in You* brilliantly demonstrates that authentic connection isn't a soft skill. Instead, it's the foundation of exceptional leadership. Michelle and Marshall provide a clear road map for leaders ready to move from transaction to connection, from control to trust, and from isolation to meaningful engagement. Read it, apply it, and watch how your leadership—and your life—transforms."

MORAG BARRETT, executive leadership coach, speaker, and bestselling author of *Cultivate* and *You, Me, We*

"*The Seismic Shift in You* captures what the highest performers already know—true influence starts from within. This book is a powerful reminder that success is not just about what you achieve, but how you lead, serve, and grow others along the way. If you're serious about unlocking your full potential and elevating those around you, this is a must-read."

DR. RUTH GOTIAN, Thinkers50 #1 Emerging Management Thinker in the World and author of *The Success Factor* and *The Financial Times Guide to Mentoring*

"In a world of uncertainty, there has never been a more important time to look inside and make sure that YOU are moving in the right direction. This book gives you all the tools to evaluate and implement a way forward to a work and life that is engaging, exciting, and fulfilling. I know—a big promise! Trust me, this book delivers! Make a seismic shift towards being a better you!"

CHESTER ELTON, bestselling author of *The Carrot Principle*, *Leading with Gratitude*, and *Anxiety at Work*

"*The Seismic Shift in You* is insightful, practical, and profoundly human. Johnston and Goldsmith show that real leadership transformation doesn't start with strategy—it starts with self-awareness. With rich stories and sharp takeaways, they make a compelling case: The best leaders lead from the inside out. If you're ready to evolve what you do *and* who you are, this is your road map."

DR. TASHA EURICH, organizational psychologist and *New York Times* bestselling author of *Shatterproof, Insight,* and *Bankable Leadership*

"As a leader in healthcare, I've seen firsthand how connection drives positive impacts—not just clinical outcomes, but team culture, trust, and empowerment. *The Seismic Shift in You* captures this truth with clarity and heart. Michelle Johnston and Marshall Goldsmith make the case that leadership today is less about control and more about authentic connection and collaboration—something we talk about often at Ochsner. If you are committed to growing as a leader who inspires others and creates lasting impact, this book serves as a valuable guide."

PETE NOVEMBER, CEO, Ochsner Health

"In a world where leadership is too often defined by titles and outcomes, Michelle Johnston and Marshall Goldsmith remind us that true influence begins with deep self-awareness and authentic connection. They lay bare a powerful truth: The most impactful leaders are the ones who are willing to look inward before leading outward."

JACQUELYN LANE AND SCOTT OSMAN, coauthors of the *Wall Street Journal* bestseller *Becoming Coachable*

MICHELLE K. JOHNSTON, PhD
MARSHALL GOLDSMITH, PhD

THE SEISMIC SHIFT IN YOU

THE SEVEN NECESSARY SHIFTS TO CREATE CONNECTION AND DRIVE RESULTS

100 COACHES
PUBLISHING
AN IMPRINT OF AMPLIFY PUBLISHING GROUP

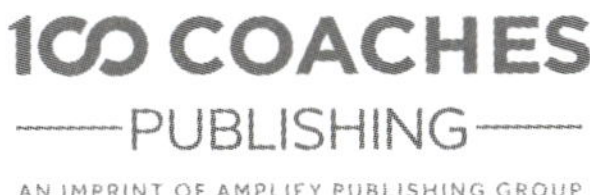

amplifypublishinggroup.com
publishing.100coaches.com

The Seismic Shift in You: The Seven Necessary Shifts to Create Connection and Drive Results

For more information, please contact:
100 Coaches Publishing, an imprint of Amplify Publishing Group
620 Herndon Parkway, Suite 220
Herndon, VA 20170
info@amplifypublishing.com

Library of Congress Control Number: 2025915111

CPSIA Code: PRV0925A

ISBN-13: 979-8-89138-621-1

Printed in the United States

The Seismic Shift in You is dedicated to my father, who is a true best practice in how positive energy is palpable, infectious, and uplifting. He shows kindness, infused with laughter, to all he meets.

And to my daughter, Elizabeth, whose beautiful spirit elevates all those around her. Keep shining brightly!

—MICHELLE

For Lyda
You are the reason behind every success I've ever known.
Your love, belief, and unwavering presence make everything possible.
I am thankful for you every single day.

—MARSHALL

CONTENTS

FOREWORD xiii

INTRODUCTION xv

CHAPTER ONE
SHIFT YOUR PERSPECTIVE 1

CHAPTER TWO
SHIFT YOUR PRIORITIES 19

CHAPTER THREE
SHIFT YOUR CALENDAR 33

CHAPTER FOUR
SHIFT YOUR MEETINGS 49

CHAPTER FIVE
SHIFT YOUR CONVERSATIONS 63

CHAPTER SIX
SHIFT YOUR LANGUAGE 79

CHAPTER SEVEN
SHIFT YOUR ENERGY 93

CONCLUSION 111

ACKNOWLEDGMENTS 119

ABOUT THE AUTHORS 121

FOREWORD

When Michelle Johnston released *The Seismic Shift in Leadership*, she reframed how we think about influence and effectiveness. Her message challenged conventional approaches to leadership by placing connection at the center of performance. In *The Seismic Shift in You,* Michelle brings the focus even closer. She speaks directly to the leader as an agent of transformation, exploring how self-awareness, presence, and daily intention shape our ability to lead others.

Across my own career, I've coached more than one hundred of the world's top CEOs—from heads of state and self-made billionaires to Olympic athletes and Fortune 500 executives. Those who sustain success are willing to do the inner work. Leadership requires more than competence—it requires clarity of self. Michelle brings this truth to life with insight and depth.

This book began as a conversation between Michelle and my longtime friend and partner Marshall Goldsmith at the Thinkers50 Awards Gala in London. That same night, I was inducted into the Thinkers50 Coaching Legends Hall of Fame, surrounded by a global community of big thinkers and bold changemakers. In that setting—at the intersection of legacy and innovation—it was clear to me: Leaders today have a responsibility not just to respond to change but to drive it—to be the architect. That's why the opening idea in this book—Shift Your Perspective—hits home. The leaders I admire most are those who ask hard questions of themselves. They challenge their assumptions. They don't wait for a crisis as a reason to grow—they choose growth as a way of leading.

Years ago, I had the privilege of meeting Maya Angelou at her home. She told me, "If you don't like something, change it. If you can't change it, change your attitude." Change isn't mere disruption—it's a decision. It's a choice, not just something that happens to you; it's a lens through which to see the world and your role in it.

If you're choosing to pick up this book, you may be seeking clarity, renewed energy, or a deeper sense of alignment. You may be navigating change or preparing to lead through it. What Michelle offers here isn't theory for its own sake. It's practical guidance rooted in years of research, coaching, teaching, and hard-earned experience. And the questions she raises will stay with you because this book doesn't ask you to become someone else. It's an invitation to reconnect with who you are and who you can become when you lead with purpose, humility, and courage.

As Maya Angelou said, "Do the best you can until you know better. Then when you know better, do better." This book will help you live—and lead—better.

Mark C. Thompson, World's #1 CEO Coach,
New York Times Bestselling Author, and Thinkers50 Coaching Hall of Fame Inductee

INTRODUCTION

In November 2023, Marshall Goldsmith and I were attending the Thinkers50 Awards Gala. Dubbed "the Oscars of management thinking" by the *Financial Times*, the event gathers some of the world's greatest minds to celebrate groundbreaking ideas in leadership, innovation, and business. I was there as part of Marshall Goldsmith's 100 Coaches group.

Marshall—my mentor and one of the most influential leadership coaches, thought leaders, and authors of our time—has left such a mark on this community that there's even an award named in his honor: the Marshall Goldsmith Distinguished Achievement Award for Coaching and Mentoring.

As I stood in the breathtaking Guildhall, a 613-year-old gothic space, I couldn't help but feel the weight of the moment. The ornate architecture seemed to hum with centuries of wisdom, making the event feel like a true collision of the past and the future—a celebration of ideas that could shape the world.

The day was filled with insights from luminaries like Dr. Amy Edmondson, Dr. Ruth Gotian, and Dorie Clark. Amy, a Harvard professor whose groundbreaking work on psychological safety is central to understanding team performance, shared how research by Google revealed a profound truth: The best teams aren't defined by technical excellence but by their ability to create safe spaces for open and honest conversations.

Ruth, a Columbia professor and expert on mentoring and achievement, reminded us of the critical role leaders play in lifting others up. To truly lead, she explained, we must guide others, mentor them, and create opportunities for their growth.

Dorie, a best-selling author and global thought leader, added her own unique perspective, leading an exercise that underscored how inclusion sits at the heart of meaningful connection. Drawing on Robbie Samuels's book *Croissants vs. Bagels*, she challenged us to stop positioning ourselves as "bagels"—closed off in tight circles—and instead be more like croissants: open, welcoming, and intentionally leaving space for others to join the conversation.

I had already written my first book, *The Seismic Shift in Leadership*, which made the case that the old ways of leading were outdated and ineffective. In it, I identified key characteristics leaders need to navigate the new world of work. As I listened to each of those top thinkers, a deeper awareness emerged: In a world increasingly shaped by AI, automation, and digital transformation, leaders must double down on what makes us distinctly human.

I realized that addressing all of the seismic changes we're experiencing requires more than technological expertise, knowledge, and awareness. To be an exceptional leader in this new landscape we find ourselves in, we must embrace a deeper shift—an *internal*, personal shift. One that involves embracing our hearts and humanity to truly pursue and embody the connection-driven leadership our world needs.

That evening, after the formal gala, Marshall and I reflected on everything we had seen and heard, including the clear call for leaders to evolve and the urgency for a deeper, internal transformation. We agreed—it's not just about what leaders do *externally*. It's about who they are and how they lead themselves first and foremost. Connection-driven leadership starts within.

"We need to write a book about this," I said to Marshall. "A book about what it takes to lead in this new landscape. Will you be my coauthor?"

Marshall smiled and said, "Let's do it."

And that was the spark for this book—a guide to leading not just with strategy and awareness but with heart and humanity. It's about how we, as leaders, can rise to meet the seismic shifts reshaping our world and how we can forge, nurture, and sustain meaningful connections—for our teams and for ourselves.

Redefining Leadership in a Disconnected Era

Maybe you've seen this scenario play out before—I see it all the time in my coaching practice.

Sam, a senior vice president at a global company, felt frustrated with the team's lack of engagement and motivation. On paper, everything looked fine. The team was filled with talented individuals, there was a clear vision, and they were consistently hitting their performance goals. But beneath the surface, something felt undeniably "off."

Meetings felt transactional. Interactions lacked energy. The sense of camaraderie and enthusiasm that had once fueled the team had all but evaporated. And the impact reached far beyond the team itself—it was affecting the entire organization.

"The energy just feels flat," Sam told me during one of our coaching sessions. "I want my team to feel excited about the work they're doing. I want them to feel proud to work for me. And honestly, I want to feel excited again too."

Sam understood that a high-performing team isn't just about hitting the numbers. It requires collaboration, connection, and shared purpose. But those essential ingredients suddenly felt out of reach. For twenty years, Sam had led with a traditional, top-down approach—but that style was no longer working.

And the disconnection wasn't limited to the team. Sam felt untethered, struggling to reconnect with a sense of purpose and identity as a senior leader. In many ways, the disconnection showing up across the organization was simply reflecting what was happening within.

Sam wasn't just searching for a way to reengage the team—but also for a way to rediscover joy, meaning, and connection in leadership.

Maybe you've felt it too. That quiet ache of going through the motions, doing everything you're supposed to do—and still wondering why it all feels so flat. The calendar is full. The work gets done. But the spark? The sense of real connection, real momentum? Missing.

I know I've felt that way before.

We live in an age where technology allows us to connect with anyone, anywhere, at any time. Yet, ironically, feelings of disconnection are more pervasive than ever.

The pandemic accelerated this paradox as remote work and digital tools blurred the lines between home and work. For Sam, the relentless "always on" culture had created a state of constant motion but little depth—a sense of being stretched thin but never truly connected.

Sam's predicament isn't unique; it's a symptom of a much larger issue: *disconnection*. Leaders across organizations are navigating a complex new reality: a workforce that's digitally connected but emotionally and socially detached. The result? Burnout, disengagement, and the unsettling realization that something fundamental is missing.

The cost of disconnection is staggering, touching every part of our lives. In 2023, U.S. Surgeon General Dr. Vivek Murthy called loneliness and social isolation a public health crisis, comparing their impact on physical health to that of smoking a pack of cigarettes every day.

I recently heard Dr. Murthy speak, and he made the case that the consequences of feeling disconnected aren't just harmful—they're *dangerous*. Loneliness doubles the likelihood of depression, increases the chance of strokes and heart attacks by 30 percent, and—most alarmingly—raises the risk of premature death by more than 60 percent.*

And this epidemic of disconnection doesn't stop at our front doors. It

* U.S. Department of Health and Human Services, "New Surgeon General Advisory Raises Alarm about the Devastating Impact of the Epidemic of Loneliness and Isolation in the United States," news release, May 3, 2023, https://www.hhs.gov/about/news/2023/05/03/new-surgeon-general-advisory-raises-alarm-about-devastating-impact-epidemic-loneliness-isolation-united-states.html.

shows up at work too. According to Gallup's *State of the Global Workplace* 2025 report, employee engagement and well-being remain below prepandemic levels—clear evidence that the workplace never fully returned to "normal." Many employees report feeling disconnected from their organization's mission and unsure whether their company even cares about them.† One in five employees says they feel lonely at work.‡

This disconnection has real consequences. When people don't feel connected, engagement drops, morale takes a hit, and burnout creeps in.

Here's something compelling: Dr. Robert Waldinger, director of the seventy-five-year Harvard Study of Adult Development, has reviewed everything from brain scans to dental records to genetic samples—and it all pointed to one key insight: "Good relationships keep us happier and healthier. Period."§

He feared the takeaway might sound too obvious. But his TED Talk sharing that truth has now been viewed over forty million times. Why? Because it confirmed what we often overlook: The greatest predictor of satisfaction and well-being isn't achievement, income, or status. It's *connection*.

Sonja Lyubomirsky's research backs this up. She found that nearly every effective happiness intervention works not because of the action itself—writing a gratitude letter, helping a friend, and so on—but because it makes us feel more connected.¶

---

† Gallup, *State of the Global Workplace: Understanding Employees, Informing Leaders* (2025), accessed June 16, 2025, https://www.gallup.com/workplace/349484/state-of-the-global-workplace.aspx.

‡ Constance Noonan Hadley and Sarah L. Wright, "We're Still Lonely at Work," *Harvard Business Review*, November 2024, https://hbr.org/2024/11/were-still-lonely-at-work.

§ Michelle Cottle, "Are We Happy Yet? The Surprising Power of Connection," *The New York Times Magazine*, May 1, 2025, https://www.nytimes.com/2025/05/01/magazine/happiness-research-studies-relationships.html.

¶ Cottle, "Are We Happy Yet?"

60%

The risk of premature death because of loneliness, isolation, and disconnection

> **"The greatest predictor of satisfaction and well-being isn't achievement, income, or status. It's CONNECTION."**
> **—DR. ROBERT WALDINGER**

So when we talk about disconnection at work, we're not just talking about productivity or engagement—we're talking about well-being, fulfillment, and satisfaction. Without meaningful relationships, even the most impressive accomplishments can feel empty.

Without connection, absenteeism rises. Turnover increases. Collaboration stalls, innovation dries up, and productivity plummets. And when leaders try to implement change—whether it's adopting new technology or navigating uncertainty—they hit resistance, not because people are unwilling but because they are unanchored.

On top of all that, the disconnection epidemic is compounded by myths that miss the mark entirely. Bringing your team back to the office doesn't automatically solve loneliness. Assigning your employees to smaller teams won't ensure meaningful bonds. And blaming loneliness on individual "neediness" ignores the critical role of leadership and work environments in fostering connection.*

The message is clear: Without meaningful connection, you struggle, your team struggles, and the entire organization struggles. But we have to understand that connection isn't transactional—it's *relational*. It's about creating workplaces where people feel seen, heard, valued, respected, and appreciated.

The good news? There is a solution. And it starts with YOU. When you make connection a priority, you create the space for your team to thrive. Because true connection builds trust, gets people engaged, and sparks the kind of collaboration that leads to real innovation.

And let me tell you, this isn't just feel-good fluff. The results are real.

---

* Hadley and Wright, "We're Still Lonely at Work."

Employees say feeling connected improves their...

- ability to do their job (60%)
- day-to-day work quality (58%)
- desire to go above and beyond (55%)
- ability to serve customers (47%)

When you make connection a priority, your teams are more satisfied, they work better together, their engagement rises, and they tend to bring their best selves to work. It's clear: Prioritizing connection transforms teams into high-performing powerhouses and fuels long-term success.

Employees say feeling connected to their work improves their ability to do their job (60 percent), day-to-day work quality (58 percent), desire to go above and beyond (55 percent), and ability to serve customers (47 percent).*

But where does this transformation begin?

The Shift Starts Within

Disconnection starts small, sneaking in through packed calendars, endless to-do lists, and the constant demands of modern life. I know this all too well. I've been there—showing up physically but mentally checked out, rushing from one meeting to the next, wondering why I feel so disengaged.

If this resonates with you, *you're not alone*. Many leaders fall into this trap, unintentionally perpetuating the very disconnection they're trying to solve.

In *The Seismic Shift in Leadership*, I shared how leaders need to move away from command-and-control habits and embrace a more connection-driven approach. That book explored the big, necessary shift that begins with reconnecting to yourself—and then ripples out to your team and organization—offering a big-picture, macro view of what it takes to lead with connection.

But here's what I've learned since: Recognizing that shift is only the beginning. To sustain it, to live it every day, you have to go deeper. You have to move past big-picture strategies and get serious about the daily, practical work of self-awareness, aligning your actions with your values

* "45% of U.S. Employees Say Organizations Aren't Investing in Fostering Employee Connection," *PR Newswire*, May 9, 2023, accessed June 2025, https://www.prnewswire.com/news-releases/45-percent-of-us-employees-say-organizations-arent-investing-in-fostering-employee-connection-301795737.html.

and intentionally creating space for the relationships that matter most.

This book takes you there. Leadership begins with the person in the mirror. No matter how innovative your organization or how talented your team, none of it will thrive if you're not first connected to yourself. That's where the seismic shift truly begins: not with a policy, a strategy, or even your team, but with YOU—with personal, daily, intentional choices that prioritize connection above all else.

Why? Because your energy, your mindset, and your presence set the tone for everything.

You can't foster trust or connection if you're running on autopilot or feeling disconnected from yourself. You can't connect with the people who matter most when your calendar is so jam-packed that you don't have time to think, let alone take bio breaks or grab lunch. You can't build safe, supportive spaces when you're weighed down by negativity—whether it's in the energy you're bringing, the thoughts you're holding, or the language you're using. And you certainly can't foster connection on your team if you rely on an authoritarian, top-down approach to leadership.

Connection needs intention, space, and openness to thrive. Without that, it just doesn't stand a chance.

On the other hand, when you choose to take ownership of your day-to-day choices—your perspective, your schedule, your meetings, and your language, for example—something powerful happens. Your presence becomes intentional. Your words carry more weight. Your actions inspire trust. Instead of reacting to every demand, you start leading from a place of focus and purpose.

The seismic shift is *personal* before it's *professional*. It begins with small, intentional changes in how you approach your thoughts, your work, your calendar, and your interactions. Though these adjustments may seem subtle, trust me—they create a ripple effect that will transform your team and your entire organization. The result? Greater engagement. Greater productivity. Happier people. More meaningful, impactful results.

This is where the journey begins: within YOU. The way you show up in your own life shapes how you show up as a leader. And the good news?

You have the power to make this shift. It's entirely within your control. All it takes is the courage to start.

The Seven Shifts That Change Everything

In this book, you're going to find clear, actionable strategies to help you rethink how you approach leadership, connection, and life. These strategies center around seven powerful shifts that will transform the way you lead and engage—both at work and in your personal life.

Drawing from over twenty-five years as a Loyola University management professor, globally recognized executive coach, keynote speaker, and host of *The Seismic Shift* podcast, I've woven in lessons and stories from incredible conversations with top thinkers, authors, leaders, and innovators. Their insights are here to inspire and guide you every step of the way.

Turn the page to find out what the seven shifts entail . . .

1 SHIFT YOUR PERSPECTIVE

The way you see leadership shapes the way you connect. When you shift your perspective—from a transactional to a connectional lens, from certainty to learning, from command to coaching, from ego to service—you unlock a deeper sense of purpose.

2 SHIFT YOUR PRIORITIES

Discover how to align your time and energy with what matters most to you. When you center your priorities around your most valued relationships, everything else falls into place.

3 SHIFT YOUR CALENDAR

Your schedule reflects your priorities. Learn how to structure your calendar to support connection, carving out time for who's most important before you fill it with everything else.

4 SHIFT YOUR MEETINGS

Transform meetings from energy-draining obligations into opportunities for meaningful dialogue. Learn how to set the tone, encourage participation, and ensure every voice is heard.

5 SHIFT YOUR CONVERSATIONS

By shifting from talking to asking great questions, you'll build trust, strengthen relationships, and create a culture where people feel seen and heard.

6 SHIFT YOUR LANGUAGE

Words matter. Understand how the language you use can empower or alienate and choose your words with intention to create meaningful connections.

7 SHIFT YOUR ENERGY

Your energy is contagious—it sets the tone for how others feel and how your team functions. Real leadership starts by being honest about the energy you're bringing and intentionally choosing how you're going to show up.

These seven shifts are the building blocks of connection, which is the foundation of effective leadership. And this book is a road map to infuse every part of your life with more connection, meaning, and *yes*—results too. Each chapter is packed with stories and practical advice to help you deepen your connections to both yourself and the people you lead.

Now, imagine walking into your next meeting and seeing it on every face in the room—each and every person feels seen, heard, valued, respected, and appreciated. They're engaged and excited to be there. Imagine a workplace where your teams are energized by a shared sense of purpose, where collaboration drives results because every person feels like they belong. Imagine the ripple effect this could have—not just on your organization's success but on your own fulfillment and the lives of everyone you touch.

This is the journey I invite you to embark upon. It's about more than hitting targets or exceeding goals; it's about showing up fully, fostering authentic connection, and creating an environment where everyone—including YOU—can thrive.

Let's get started. The seismic shift in YOU begins now.

SHIFT YOUR PERSPECTIVE

How do YOU view leadership?

When you shift your perspective from a transactional to a connection-based mindset, you unlock a deeper sense of purpose.

CHAPTER ONE

SHIFT YOUR PERSPECTIVE

"Leadership is not about executive position or title. It is about connection and influence. At its highest, leadership is all about adding value to the world and blessing lives through the work you do."

—ROBERT S. SHARMA

I can't tell you how many times I found myself in tears—frustrated, overwhelmed, exhausted—in my first five years as a professor.

The world of academia felt like a hostile place. A place I didn't really feel like I belonged. I desperately wanted to achieve tenure, but to get there, I needed glowing faculty evaluations. My dean made that crystal clear.

And mine? They were the exact opposite of glowing.

In fact, my students were straight-up calling me a b%@$#.

And you know what? I don't blame them. I was rigid and demanding. I kept a strict wall between me and my students—all business, no personality, rarely ever sharing anything about my personal life. Not because that's who I was deep down, but because that's how I thought I had to act to be successful.

When I started at Loyola, I was a twenty-eight-year-old professor teaching MBA students, many of them older than me. I hadn't even finished

**Jerk bosses are out.
Connected leaders are in.**

my dissertation yet, and I was desperate to prove myself. So I ran my classroom like a drill sergeant, convinced that power, control, and authority were the only ways to earn respect.

The problem? It wasn't me.

Before academia, I'd worked in consulting. I knew that people learned best through experiential learning. I had led workshops all over the country where connection, interaction, and engagement made all the difference. But when I stepped into the classroom, I suppressed all of that. I ignored what I knew about how people actually learn because I was so focused on fitting in and being taken seriously.

And this approach failed . . . *miserably*.

I was in the process of trying to figure out how to improve my faculty evaluations when I picked up the book *The Art of Possibility* by Benjamin Zander. Zander, former conductor of the Boston Philharmonic Orchestra, talked about how he had spent years leading with control, believing his role was to dictate and correct with his all-powerful baton.

But then he realized something startling—he had inadvertently created a culture of fear. His musicians weren't playing at their best. They were scared of him. Scared of making mistakes. Instead of feeling inspired, they were holding back. And fear, of course, stifles both creativity and excellence.

So he flipped his perspective.

He decided that instead of seeing his musicians as people who needed to be corrected, he would see them all as "A" students—all capable of excellence. His job? To help them get there. To help them realize and achieve their excellence.

As I thought about how Zander was running things, I had an epiphany.

Oh. My. God.

That was *me*.

I had built the same culture in my classroom. I had been so focused on proving myself and maintaining power and control that I was creating fear in the very people I was supposed to be developing. I was stifling their excellence! And I certainly wasn't playing to my strengths.

I had been so focused on proving myself and maintaining power and control that I was creating fear in the very people I was supposed to be developing.

I wasn't the kind of professor who wanted to intimidate students into learning. I was a coach. A cheerleader. An enthusiastic champion of people. That's who I've always been.

And yet, I had buried all of that under the weight of trying to be "successful" by someone else's definition.

That realization absolutely transformed my perspective on leadership.

The next semester, I walked into my class on day one and told my students, "Everything you've heard about me? It's changing. I'm doing things differently. My job is to help you succeed. From now on, I see myself as your coach. I would love it if every single one of you earned an A by the end of the semester. If you work with me—if we do this together—we'll get there. But here's what I need from you . . ."

I made it clear: They had to show up. They had to engage. They had to put in the work. And in return? I was going to do everything in my power to get them across the finish line.

And guess what? It worked!

The energy in my classroom completely shifted. My students leaned in. They asked questions; they took risks; they engaged. I was connecting with them. And I actually started enjoying teaching. It was *fun*.

The best part of all was that I was leading in a way that felt right. I wasn't *performing* leadership anymore. I wasn't trying to be someone I wasn't. I was showing up as me, and I was happier for it.

The cherry on top? I received tenure and was named Faculty Member of the Year. Talk about a transformation, right?

Listen, I know what it's like to think that power and control are the only ways to get results. I also know what happens when you finally let that go—when you shift your perspective and start leading in a way that actually prioritizes connection.

And that perspective shift? It has to come first.

So let's start there. Let's shift how YOU view leadership. Because once you do, everything else gets a whole lot easier.

The Seismic Shift in Perspective

Let's be real—when you step into leadership, no one hands you a manual titled *Here's Exactly How to Do This Leadership Thing*. There's no map. No guide. No step-by-step foolproof process.

So what do we do? We rely on what we know. We try to minimize what we don't. We lean on our expertise, focus on getting things right, and hope no one notices we're winging it.

And somewhere along the way, without meaning to, we start to believe that great leadership means knowing it all. That our value comes from having all the answers. From never making mistakes. From being in control at all times.

Makes sense, right? The higher you climb, the greater the expectations. More people look to you for guidance. You're responsible for bigger decisions, bigger results, bigger *everything*. The pressure is real. And the margin for error? It feels smaller and smaller.

But here's where that perspective backfires: When leadership becomes about *you*—your expertise, your authority, your need to get it right—you can so easily lose sight of the people you're leading. You can get so focused on control that you forget about trust. You can spend more time trying to prove yourself than developing others.

When leadership becomes about *you*—your expertise, your authority, your need to get it right—you can so easily lose sight of the people you're leading.

Suddenly, leadership isn't something you do with people. It's something you do *alone*.

Here's the problem with that: Leadership is about people. And people are hardwired for connection. Whether you realize it or not, connection isn't just *a* leadership skill—it's *the* leadership skill. It's what makes you effective. It's what fuels engagement. It's what turns good teams into great ones.

And it's more important now than ever.

Gone are the days when we tolerated toxic bosses and suffocating work cultures—we aren't going to stick around for leaders who don't get us, who don't see us, who don't appreciate us. We want more. We want purpose. We want meaning. We want to be seen as full humans. We want balance, fulfillment, and yes—*connection*.

If you want to attract and retain top talent, if you want to lead in a way that actually works, if you want leadership to feel more fulfilling—you have to shift your perspective.

Leadership isn't about standing at the top of the mountain shouting directions. It's about being on the climb *with* your people, creating an environment where they feel seen, valued, and empowered to do their best work.

This shift in perspective changes everything.

A Connection-First Perspective

I laughed out loud when Garry Ridge told me how he used to introduce himself from the stage: "G'day." (He's Australian.) "I'm Garry Ridge. I'm the consciously incompetent, probably wrong, and roughly right chairman and CEO of WD-40 Company, and I need all the help I can get."

How likable is this guy? And yes, he really *is* that chipper in real life.

As CEO of WD-40 Company, he liked to say the board had taken a chance on "some dumbass from Australia"—someone who'd never set foot on Wall Street but was passionate about sharing that iconic blue-and-yellow can with the world.

Classic Garry—self-deprecating, lighthearted, and completely unafraid to laugh at himself. But underneath that humor is something deeper: a belief that leadership isn't about *him*—it's about the people he serves.

Early on, Garry came across two quotes that grounded his entire approach to leadership:

> *"Our purpose in life is to make people happy. If we can't make them happy, at least don't hurt them."*
> —Dalai Lama

> *"Pleasure in the job puts perfection in the work."*
> —Aristotle

That was it. *That* was the kind of workplace he wanted to build. A place where people didn't just show up but *wanted* to be there. A place where people felt valued, trusted, and empowered to do great work.

Don't you want to work in a place like that?

Here's what made Garry different: Instead of assuming he already had the answers, he went back to school.

As a publicly traded company's CEO, he enrolled in a two-year master's program in leadership. He studied under Dr. Ken Blanchard, a pioneer in servant leadership, and took everything he learned back to WD-40 Company.

And then he started making changes.

WD-40 ditched the title "manager" and replaced it with "coach." That single change spoke volumes. Because great coaches don't micromanage. They don't hoard knowledge. They don't make it all about them.

Instead, they equip. They encourage. They challenge.

A coach doesn't run onto the field and take the ball. They may step in to guide the play, but they don't take over. They spend most of their time observing, offering feedback, and helping players improve. And when the team wins, they celebrate with their people.

Garry also knew that connection and trust don't happen from a distance. They happen in the trenches. So instead of staying in the executive suite, he spent time where it mattered most—in what he called the "stinky locker room." He made it clear that he was in it with his people. That's where real leadership happens. That's where trust is built.

And here's where Garry really flipped the script: He refused to call mistakes failures. Instead, he called them "learning moments."

Think about that for a second.

What would happen if your organization stopped seeing mistakes as things to avoid or punish and started seeing them as opportunities to learn? How much more innovative would your team be? How much more engaged?

What would happen if your organization stopped seeing mistakes as things to avoid or punish and started seeing them as opportunities to learn?

Fear of failure is one of the most disabling emotions in business. WD-40 took that fear off the table entirely. They even stopped using the word "failure" altogether.

No lying. No faking. No hiding.

And the results? They speak for themselves.

Even when I asked Garry how he was feeling about his latest book, *Any Dumb-Ass Can Do It*, his answer had nothing to do with personal success.

He told me he felt fulfilled—not because he wrote the book but because he wanted the content of the book to be a gift to leaders. He wanted to share all that he had learned in his twenty-five years as the CEO of WD-40 Company.

"Happy people create happy families. Happy families create happy communities. And happy communities create a happier world," he said. "Leaders in business have the biggest opportunity to influence happiness in people's lives because going to work takes up so much time."

Garry built an entire company around this perspective. It turns out putting people first isn't just good for morale. It's great for business. During his tenure:

- WD-40 Company's market cap grew significantly.
- They expanded the blue-and-yellow can with the little red top into 176 countries.
- During the Great Resignation—what Garry calls the "Great Escape"—while countless companies struggled to retain employees, WD-40 Company maintained a 93 percent engagement rate.

Garry understands that when people feel valued, trusted, and connected, they're happier. And happy people work harder. They do better work. They also go home feeling fulfilled and bring that energy to their families and their communities.

Shift your perspective and you'll see what he saw: Connection drives results—personally and professionally. And connecting with others brings greater fulfillment to everything you do.

Marshall on Shifting Your Perspective

Believe me, I know what you might be thinking.

Maybe you're reading this and thinking, *I'm just not wired that way. That connection-first leadership stuff? That's not me. I've never been that kind of leader.*

By the time most people reach senior leadership, they've developed a polished story about how they operate—what works for them, what doesn't, what they're "just not good at." It feels like self-awareness. But often, it's just a fixed perspective we've stopped questioning.

In *The Seismic Shift in Leadership*, Michelle challenged leaders to examine the stories they've been living out and ask, *Is this story still serving me? Or is it quietly holding me back?*

Leadership isn't about standing at the top of the mountain shouting directions. It's about being on the climb *with* your people, creating an environment where they feel seen, heard, and empowered to do their best work.

That work—of updating your story—is foundational.

In today's world, where connection is the currency of effective leadership, you have to be willing to shift your story.

You have to be willing to ask whether the perspective you've been leading from—perhaps rooted in control, certainty, or self-protection—is getting in the way of the connection your team needs most.

You've probably heard a few of these. Maybe even said them yourself:

"I don't have time to get personal."

"I'm not good with people."

"My results speak for themselves."

"Connection just isn't my thing."

We say these things with a shrug, a sheepish smile, or an air of resignation. "Sorry," we offer, "that's just the way I am."

But here's the truth: That's not the way you are. That's just the way you've *told yourself* you are.

And if your goal is to lead more effectively in today's world, then holding on to that story isn't just limiting—it's costly.

These offhand statements may sound harmless, but over time, they quietly sabotage your growth and your ability to connect.

What makes these stories so tricky is how reasonable they sound. It feels like we're being honest, like we're owning who we are. But more often, we're just rehearsing old narratives that were written years ago by parents, teachers, siblings, or even younger versions of ourselves. And we've been repeating those lines ever since.

These aren't facts. They're beliefs. And beliefs are just perspectives we've practiced over and over again.

As a coach, I've worked with countless brilliant, high-performing people who carry around outdated labels like tattoos. But the truth is, very few of our so-called flaws are hardwired. Tardiness, a quick temper, chronic procrastination, poor communication—these aren't genetic conditions. They're habits. And habits can change.

I once worked with a client who told me, "I can't listen. I've never been able to."

I smiled and asked, "Do you have a medical condition that prevents you from hearing words?"

He laughed. "No."

So I followed up: "If someone had a gun to your head and said, 'Start listening, or else,' would you listen?"

Of course, he said yes. He could listen. He just hadn't practiced it—because he'd bought into a story that made it easier not to try.

Another client told me, "I can't give recognition. I've never been good at that."

So I asked, "Would recognizing someone improve their performance? Would it make them feel more valued? Does it cost you anything?"

He paused. Thought about it. Then admitted the issue wasn't ability—it was effort. It was choice. He hadn't been born without the recognition gene. He had simply never made it a priority.

And in that moment, what he really did was shift his perspective—from limitation to possibility. From control to connection.

I know this personally too.

I grew up in Valley Station, Kentucky—a small town where the odds of becoming a best-selling author were slim to none. We didn't have much. In fact, we didn't even have indoor plumbing when I started school. But what I did have was a mother who believed in me.

She was a first-grade teacher who stayed home to raise me, and she poured her energy into shaping my future. From the time I was little, she repeated one message over and over again: "*You are smart. You are smart. You are so smart.*"

And I believed her. That belief became the cornerstone of my identity. Her voice became my inner voice, and it pushed me toward goals that might've seemed impossible otherwise.

But she didn't stop there.

She also told me, "You have no mechanical skills. You'll never have any."

She wasn't being cruel. She just didn't want me to follow in my father's footsteps and spend my life working with my hands at a gas station. She wanted more for me. But just as I had absorbed the idea that I was smart, I also absorbed the belief that I wasn't mechanical—and I never questioned it.

So I avoided tools. I steered clear of anything that required building, fixing, or understanding how things worked. I didn't practice. I didn't learn. I didn't try.

I once scored in the bottom 2 percent on the army's mechanical aptitude test. I failed a mechanical exercise in graduate school. And every time, I shrugged it off with a laugh: "Well, I'm just not mechanical."

But eventually, that belief started to feel less like a harmless quirk and more like a wall I had built around myself.

At twenty-six, I finally stopped and asked myself: *Why can I solve complex math problems but not hammer a nail?*

The answer wasn't ability. It wasn't wiring. It was perspective.

I hadn't been born without mechanical skills. I had just been told I didn't have them—and I believed that story.

We do the same thing with leadership.

We tell ourselves we're too analytical to connect . . . too busy to build trust . . . too "results-driven" to care about feelings.

But those aren't facts. They're filters. And if we don't challenge them, we keep leading from a place of limitation rather than connection.

So what if "*That's just the way I am*" became "*That's something I'm working on*"? What if, instead of defending your limitations, you got curious about your potential?

We weren't born with these identities. We inherited them. We rehearsed them. And now, we get to rewrite them.

So ask yourself:

- *What belief about leadership is keeping you from connecting?*
- *What story are you defending that might no longer be true?*

- *What might shift if you chose a new perspective—one rooted in trust, connection, and possibility?*

How to See Leadership Differently

If you've spent years believing you need to be the expert, the authority, the one with the right answer every time, letting go of that mindset can feel risky and uncomfortable. But the truth is, the best leaders aren't the ones who command the room. They're the ones who create space for others to excel.

Ready to shift your perspective on leadership? Here's where to start.

1 START BY CHALLENGING THE STORY

Take a moment and think about the story you've been telling yourself about the kind of leader you are. Maybe it's something like "I'm not great with people" or "I've just never been the warm-and-fuzzy type." Those stories might feel like facts—but often, they're just familiar scripts we've repeated without question. What if you pressed pause on that narrative? What if, instead of deciding what you're not, you got curious about who you're becoming?

2 TRADE CERTAINTY FOR LEARNING

You don't have to be the smartest person in the room. In fact, if you are, you're in the wrong room. The best leaders never stop learning. Instead of trying to prove what you know, get curious about what you don't. Take a page from Garry Ridge—he was running a billion-dollar company and still went back to school to study leadership. What would happen if you approached your role with that same openness? If you made it less about having all the answers and more about finding them—together?

3 TRUST RATHER THAN CONTROL

Micromanaging isn't leadership. It's exhaustion—for both you and your people. If you want your team to take ownership, you have to let go. Set the vision. Define the expectations. And then? Step back. Give your team space to rise to the challenge. Trust them before they've "earned" it, and they'll show you why they deserve it.

4 COACH INSTEAD OF COMMAND

Think about the best leader you've ever worked with. Were they the kind of person who barked orders and demanded compliance? Or did they challenge you, encourage you, and help you grow? That's the shift. Your team doesn't need a taskmaster—they need a coach. Someone who listens. Someone who believes in them. Someone who's willing to give real feedback.

5 MAKE FAILURE A LEARNING MOMENT

No one does their best work when they're terrified of messing up. If people are afraid to fail, they'll play it safe. And safe doesn't lead to breakthroughs. So stop treating mistakes like disasters and start treating them like data. When something doesn't go as planned, ask, *What can we learn?* Do that enough, and your team won't just get better—they'll get bolder.

6 PUT PEOPLE FIRST—ALWAYS

At the end of the day, leadership is about making people feel valued. It's about creating an environment where people want to show up because they know they matter. So instead of asking, *How can I succeed?* try asking, *How can I help my team succeed?* When you do that—when you make leadership about them, not you—everything changes.

Shift your perspective, and the results will follow. But more than that? Leadership will feel different. Lighter. More fulfilling. More fun. And isn't that the point?

YOUR CHALLENGE

Make a Seismic Shift in Your Perspective

Notice where certainty is getting in the way of connection. Where are you gripping too tightly? Is there a decision where you're clinging to control instead of trusting your team? Are you in a situation where the fear of failure is holding you back from trying something new? Pick one place to shift. Let go of the need to have all the answers and lean into learning. Swap control for trust. Stop avoiding mistakes and start looking for the lesson. Put on your coaching hat and get into the stinky locker room with your people.

SHIFT YOUR PRIORITIES

Do you align your time and energy with what matters the most?

When you center your priorities around YOUR most valued relationships, including yourself, everything else falls into place.

CHAPTER TWO

SHIFT YOUR PRIORITIES

"What if we stopped celebrating being busy as a measurement of importance? What if instead we celebrated how much time we had spent listening, pondering, meditating, and enjoying time with the most important people in our lives?"

—GREG McKEOWN
Essentialism: The Disciplined Pursuit of Less

The house glowed with holiday lights, the stockings were hung, and my daughter Elizabeth was home from college—I was thrilled! My calendar was packed with festive gatherings, and by all accounts, it should have been a season of joy. But something felt off. No matter how much I tried to embrace the holiday spirit, I couldn't shake this undercurrent of disconnection.

It wasn't a feeling I'd carried all year. In fact, most of the year had been filled with meaningful moments that had energized me. But as December unfolded, my usual rhythm had been disrupted. The weeks leading up to the holidays were a blur of back-to-back Zoom calls, last-minute podcast recordings, and end-of-year deadlines. The rituals that kept me connected—Monday morning coffee group, walks in the park with friends, regular Pilates classes and pickleball games—had disappeared.

Instead, the holiday hustle had taken over.

Then one evening, Elizabeth looked at me and said, "Mom, I've been home for two weeks, and I've barely seen you."

Her words hit me like a gut punch. How had I let this happen? The person who mattered most to me—my number one priority—was right in front of me, and I'd been too caught up in the end-of-the-year busyness to be fully present. I was thrilled to have her home, yet I hadn't slowed down enough to savor our time together.

The irony wasn't lost on me. I teach the importance of connection, yet there I was, falling into the same reactive patterns I caution others about. I hadn't been intentionally prioritizing the moments that mattered most, and it took my daughter's words to snap me out of it. I knew exactly what I needed to do. That Friday before Christmas, I shut my laptop, cleared my schedule for two weeks, and made space for what truly mattered.

It's easy—for all of us—to get swept up in what feels urgent. But in that rush, we often lose sight of what's most important: connection with ourselves and with those we love. My holiday season was overwhelming not because I didn't love my work—I had simply let busyness take precedence over the things that fuel me. And in the process, my connection with myself had suffered.

This is a very important shift. To be a connection-driven leader, you have to start by reconnecting with yourself. When we prioritize things that fuel us, we show up differently. We lead differently. We live differently.

To be a connection-driven leader, you have to start by reconnecting with yourself. When we prioritize things that fuel us, we show up differently. We lead differently. We live differently.

The Seismic Shift in Priorities

As I reflected on my own wake-up call, I kept coming back to a conversation I'd had with Chantell Preston on my podcast. A powerhouse healthcare entrepreneur, Chantell has built an incredible career while championing authenticity, resilience, and growth—especially for women in leadership. But what stood out most to me in our time together was her deep connection with herself and the clarity she had gained through hard-earned experience.

Chantell shared a defining moment that forced her to reevaluate everything. On the very day she finalized the sale of her company—a milestone she had poured years into—her partner unexpectedly served her divorce papers. She had spent so much time chasing professional success, believing financial security would create the future she wanted for her family. Instead, she found herself standing at the finish line with everything she thought she wanted—except the person who mattered most.

That moment changed everything.

She had sacrificed the everyday moments—the milestones in her child's life, the irreplaceable time with loved ones. She had built something big but lost sight of what made life meaningful. It forced her to pause and ask: *What am I really building?*

The shift didn't happen overnight, but Chantell committed to the long haul. She started treating her priorities as a mirror of her values. Instead of filling every available moment, she became fiercely protective of the people and experiences that brought her joy. Success was no longer about doing more but about aligning her life with what mattered most.

This realization has shaped her work ever since, including her podcast *Get Real, Get Results*, where she challenges the myth of work–life balance. Chantell will tell you: Balance doesn't exist. What does exist is integration. Work and life constantly overlap. The real question is: *How do you design your life to reflect what matters most—right now, in this season?*

This is the seismic shift in priorities—moving from a place where you react to everything that pops up to a place where you intentionally choose what matters most to YOU.

So, let me ask you: *How often do you find yourself at the bottom of your own priority list?*

If you're like most leaders, it happens more than you'd like to admit. You spend your days juggling responsibilities, responding to urgent demands, and making sure everyone else's needs are met. And somewhere in the chaos, your own well-being fades into the background.

It's easy to fall into a reactive mode, especially in high-pressure roles. But here's the truth: When you're constantly putting yourself last, you're not leading at your best. You're drained, disconnected, and running on fumes. Prioritizing yourself isn't selfish. It's quite the opposite. When you align your time and energy with what truly matters to you, you're better equipped to show up fully for the people and work that depend on you. In other words, when you care for yourself, you're in a better position to care for others.

When you align your time and energy with what truly matters to you, you're better equipped to show up fully for the people and work that depend on you. When you care for yourself, you're in a better position to care for others.

Best of Me

When I first met Taylor Johnson, I had no idea how much I needed his guidance. I was doing work I loved—coaching executives, giving speeches, running the Saints and Pelicans Leadership Academy, and taking a sabbatical from Loyola to write this book.

But somewhere along the way, I had lost sight of how to prioritize myself. My calendar was packed, my energy was scattered, and I felt more like a pinball bouncing around a loud and blinking machine than a steady leader in control of my own life.

I was depleted. Absolutely empty.

Enter Taylor—a former NFL performance coach turned executive performance coach. He specializes in helping leaders build systems that align their time, energy, and values to unlock their potential, confidence, and capacity. He didn't ask me to squeeze more into my already-overloaded schedule or push hyperproductivity. His approach was about clarity—getting clear on what truly mattered and structuring my days in a way that supported my best self.

He calls it the "Winning Formula," and it's grounded in one essential truth: You can't show up for others if you're not showing up for yourself.

Taylor started by helping me reconnect with myself—beginning with self-awareness. He guided me through an exercise reflecting on three distinct eras of my life: my twenties, my thirties, and my forties. For each one, he asked thoughtful questions: *What brought you joy during that time? Who supported you? What drained your energy? What values, beliefs, and behaviors showed up the most?*

As I answered the same questions across the decades, patterns began to emerge. I saw clearly that I'm energized by collaboration, connection, and creativity—and dragged down by negativity, judgmental thinking, and closed environments. I noticed that whenever my work, relationships, and personal growth weren't aligned, I lost connection with myself—and, as a result, with the people and work that mattered most.

Through that reflection, I gained clarity on my personal formula for success: what's been effective, what still serves me, and, most importantly, what no longer does.

Then Taylor asked, "What does your best day look like?"

I told him it starts with exercise—that's when I feel the most energized, clearheaded, and ready to take on the day. His response: "Hold that time sacred. Protect it like you would an important meeting, and don't let anyone take it away."

I realized that, even when I scheduled that time for myself, if a client or a friend needed me, I would always say yes. I thought I was doing the right thing. In reality, I was draining myself. I wasn't holding the things that mattered to me sacred, and that was one of the biggest reasons I had ended up depleted in the first place.

I wasn't holding the things that mattered to me sacred, and that was one of the biggest reasons I had ended up depleted in the first place.

From there, we dug deeper. "What else makes you feel like your best self?" he asked.

For me, it was shopping with my daughter, walking in the park with friends, and creating content for my speeches, workshops, and podcast.

This led me to Taylor's *Best of Me* framework—an exercise designed to clarify the conditions that allow me to thrive. Inspired by Daniel Coyle's *The Culture Playbook*, it invited two reflections:

- I'm at my best when . . .
- I'm at my worst when . . .

This framework helped me identify what fuels me—and what drains me. From there, we mapped out three key areas of connection to prioritize:

- **SELF:** How do I nurture my own well-being through exercise, creativity, and rest?
- **OTHERS:** Who are the most important people in my personal and professional lives, and how do I make time for them?
- **COMMUNITY:** What groups or shared spaces bring me a sense of belonging and purpose?

Taylor also introduced me to *stack ranking*—ordering priorities by importance. Knowing what matters is one thing; structuring your time around it is another. He challenged me to ask myself: *Does my calendar reflect my values?* The answer was a hard no (more on that in the next chapter!). I had been saying yes to everything at a great cost to myself, and that lack of alignment was eroding my ability to connect—both with myself and with the world around me.

I had been saying yes to everything at a great cost to myself, and that lack of alignment was eroding my ability to connect—both with myself and with the world around me.

Connection starts with YOU. When you're clear on your priorities and commit to what fuels you, you can show up fully for the people and work that matter most to you. Taking care of yourself allows everything else to fall into place. Without that internal alignment, you end up running on empty, offering only fragments of yourself instead of the full, engaged version of who you are.

Marshall on Shifting Your Priorities

Michelle makes an important point: Clarifying what fuels you—what really matters—is essential. And she's right. Building on that, the next step is asking: *Are you actually living those priorities?*

In my experience, this is where so many leaders struggle. They don't lack insight. They aren't short on good intentions. But when the demands pile up and the pressure is on, they default to habit. They get busy. And without meaning to, they lose alignment between what they say matters and what they actually choose to focus on.

So how do you close that gap? How do you make sure your priorities aren't just words—but the foundation of how you lead and live?

One of my clients, Jorge Gonzalez, the CEO of City National Bank in

Connection starts with YOU. When you're clear on your priorities and commit to what fuels you, you can show up fully for the people and work that matter most to you. Taking care of yourself allows everything else to fall into place.

Miami, has found a powerful way to help leaders wrestle with this question. He's someone who constantly challenges his team to think bigger—not just about performance but about purpose. Even when business is thriving, he urges his leaders to ask, "How can we do even better?"

And Jorge does something that more leaders should do: He builds habits and practices that hold himself and his team accountable to their priorities.

He introduced us to an exercise that we now use with leaders at every level. It's simple. It's powerful. And—most importantly—it forces clarity on whether your choices reflect your priorities.

Step 1: The Bonus Round

Start by asking this question: *"If you were given two bonus hours per week to do whatever you believe would be in the best long-term interest of the company, how would you spend this time?"*

When leaders are asked this question, their posture changes. Their eyes light up. It's as if someone has unlocked a door they forgot existed. Ideas pour out—visionary, energizing, creative.

And two themes consistently rise to the top:

1. **CREATING THE ORGANIZATION OF THE FUTURE**
   Leaders talk about strategic planning, innovation, thinking long-term—not just solving today's problems but imagining tomorrow's possibilities. Yet ironically, these future-shaping conversations are often the first to get pushed aside when schedules get packed. Which means the most important work rarely gets the time it truly deserves.

2. **DEVELOPING THE LEADERS OF THE FUTURE**
   Nearly every leader mentions the joy and impact of mentoring others. They speak with pride about helping people grow, knowing

it strengthens the company and brings meaning to their own leadership.

These are not pipe dreams. They're aspirations rooted in value. They're priorities. But here's the tension: If these activities matter so much, why aren't they already happening?

Step 2: The Elimination Game

Now, on to the next question: *"If you were forced to eliminate two hours of your current workload, what would you stop doing?"*

This is where leaders identify where those two hours can come from. They identify meetings that don't serve a purpose, tasks they've been doing out of habit, or work they could confidently delegate.

And then, just as quickly, comes the pushback: *"This sounds great, but what will my manager think?"*

Which brings us to step three.

Step 3: The Alignment Conversation

Leaders are encouraged to sit down with their managers and share what they'd like to add to their workloads as well as what they'd like to eliminate. Some suggestions get fine-tuned. But more often than not, managers respond with support. They appreciate the thoughtfulness. They're encouraged by the initiative.

Because this isn't about doing less—it's about doing what matters more.

This exercise may sound small. But it's not. It's a reorientation—a way of checking whether your actions match your intentions.

We often assume that aligning with our priorities requires major disruption, bold declarations, or sweeping strategy shifts. But sometimes, the most powerful move you can make is to reclaim two hours. Two hours that were drifting. Two hours that could be invested in people, purpose, and future impact.

Because at the end of the day, your priorities aren't what you *say* they are. Your priorities are what you choose—again and again.

How to Prioritize Connection with Yourself

If you're running on empty, distracted by the next task, or saying yes to everything at the expense of what fills you up, it's impossible to show up fully for the people and work that matter most. Meaningful connection with others starts with a strong connection to yourself.

So, how do you make yourself a priority in a way that feels intentional and sustainable?

Here are a few ways to start:

1 IDENTIFY WHAT MATTERS MOST

Take a moment to reflect on what's truly important in your life. Taylor's framework emphasizes intentional prioritization to add clarity to your life. What are the relationships, activities, or commitments that matter most to you? What are the top contenders that give you energy? Write them down and ask yourself: *Are these priorities reflected in how I spend my time?*

2 RANK YOUR PRIORITIES

Not everything can be your number one. Taylor's advice is to list your priorities in order of importance. This exercise forces you to make choices. What comes first—your health, your family, your creative work? Knowing your top priorities helps you focus your energy where it's most needed instead of spreading yourself too thin.

3 START WITH YOUR NONNEGOTIABLES

What are the activities that make you feel like your best self? Maybe it's exercise, learning something new, or preparing healthy family dinners. Make those *nonnegotiables*. These are the anchors in your day or week that support your well-being. Protect them fiercely; hold them sacred.

4 ASSESS WHAT'S DRAINING YOU

Prioritizing also involves letting go. What's pulling your attention away from the most important things? Look at the tasks, commitments, or relationships that consistently drain you. Ask yourself if they align with your priorities. If not, consider how you can outsource, reduce, or eliminate them.

5 REVISIT YOUR PRIORITIES REGULARLY

Life changes, and so do your priorities. Set aside time each month or quarter to reflect on what's working and what's not. Are you still aligned with your values? Are there new priorities emerging? This ongoing practice ensures you stay connected with yourself and avoid slipping back into reactive mode.

6 CHECK FOR ALIGNMENT

As Marshall often reminds leaders, your priorities aren't what you say they are—they're what you consistently choose. Take a moment to ask yourself: *If I had two bonus hours each week, how would I spend them?* Your answer will tell you a lot about what truly matters—and whether your current choices reflect it. Then, take the next step and ask yourself, *If I were forced to eliminate two hours of my current workload, what would I stop doing?* Then—make it happen.

When you're clear on your priorities, you stop making decisions out of obligation and start making them from a place of alignment. You move through your day with more energy, more presence, and more connection—not just with yourself but with everyone around you.

YOUR CHALLENGE

Make a Seismic Shift in Your Priorities

Choose three ways to realign your time with what fuels you. Maybe it's protecting your morning workout, saying no to something that drains you, or making space for coffee with someone who fills your cup. Write down your top three priorities and keep them where you'll see them. When something new comes up, pause and ask: *Does this align with what is most important in this season?* If not, give yourself permission to say no.

SHIFT YOUR CALENDAR

Does your calendar reflect your priorities?

Structuring YOUR calendar to support connection reduces unnecessary busyness.

CHAPTER THREE

SHIFT YOUR CALENDAR

"The key is not to prioritize what is on your schedule, but to schedule your priorities."

—STEPHEN R. COVEY

Most of us would say certain relationships—family, friends, coworkers—are a priority. Does your calendar actually reflect that? Don't be fooled—this chapter isn't about time management. It's about making space in your calendar—intentionally, rhythmically, and consistently—for the people who matter most. We're going to talk about how to use your calendar as a powerful tool to nurture connection and keep your most important relationships strong.

When my daughter Elizabeth was six weeks old, a friend told me about a playgroup for moms with babies the same age. Even though I was a working mom, my teaching schedule at Loyola gave me just enough flexibility to join the gatherings when I wasn't in the classroom.

Once a week, we got together with our babies in each other's homes, swapping stories about sleep schedules, first steps, and the endless cycle of ear infections. It was a lifeline—one that carried us through toddlerhood, preschool drop-offs, and the transition into full-time school.

But as our kids grew, our gatherings became less frequent. A few of us kept up with occasional lunches, but without something structured, time together kept slipping through the cracks. We all felt it—that slow drift. So we gathered a few from the original group and set a new rhythm: a monthly coffee date. And for a while, that worked.

Until the pandemic hit.

But in the midst of all that uncertainty, we realized just how much we needed each other. So we made a decision: Every Monday morning at eight a.m., we would meet. We started in backyards, bundled up with coffees in hand. And when the lockdown was lifted and the world opened up again, we kept the rhythm going. Same day, same time, every single week.

On paper, Monday at eight a.m. is a terrible time for a group of busy moms. But that's what makes it work. There's no endless back-and-forth trying to "find a time that works for everyone"—this *is* the time. Whoever can make it shows up. No guilt. No pressure.

Some weeks, there are nine of us. Other weeks, just a handful. But no matter what, every single week, we gather for an hour over coffee and pass a spoon around. Whoever holds the spoon shares their update—whether it's laughter over a kid's latest antics, tears over an empty nest, or the unexpected weight of this season of life. And when someone says, "I need help," we show up.

I recently saw Charles Duhigg speak at a book festival about his *New York Times* best-selling book *Supercommunicators*. He said something powerful about our needs when communicating. He said humans want one of three things when interacting:

1. We want to be helped.
2. We want to be heard.
3. Or we want to be hugged.

But we need to ask for what we want. This coffee group has become a space where we do exactly that. Sometimes we'd like advice. Sometimes we want to share an update on our life. And sometimes we just need some shoulders to cry on.

Over the years, we've supported each other through the challenging teenage years, college applications, aging parents, and personal losses. We've been there through sicknesses, job changes, divorces, and life pivots. But most importantly, we've been intentional about embedding this time into our calendars. Because if we hadn't? It never would've lasted.

And let me tell you, this one hour with these women is just as critical to my well-being as anything I do for work. They are my friends, my advisors, my sounding boards, the people I turn to when I need perspective. They're the ones who showed up for me during my divorce, who greeted guests at my book launch, and who remind me—week after week—that I'm never alone in this journey.

And here's what I've learned: Saying relationships are a priority for you is one thing. Embedding those important relationships into your calendar is another thing. Making time and consistently showing up create the pathway to connection.

Saying relationships are a priority for you is one thing. Embedding those important relationships into your calendar is another thing.

Without this ritual built into all of our calendars, it would be easy to drift apart, to let busyness take over. And then, in a time of crisis, we'd have to scramble to find support. But because we've made this a priority—because it's part of our weekly rhythm—our support system is strong.

So, what about you?

When it comes to relationships, it's not just about knowing who matters to you—it's about making time for them. Let's talk about moving from intention to action—shifting your calendar to reflect your priorities.

The Seismic Shift in Your Calendar

In the last chapter, we focused on the most important relationship in your life—the one with yourself. We talked about what fuels you, what keeps you grounded, and how to prioritize the habits, routines, and moments that help you show up as your best self.

But connection—even with yourself—extends beyond you. It's about the people who make your life richer—the relationships that sustain you, challenge you, and lift you up. And just like with your own well-being, if those relationships don't hold space in your calendar, they're not actually a priority.

Connection—even with yourself—extends beyond you. It's about the people who make your life richer—the relationships that sustain you, challenge you, and lift you up.

When Marshall was writing *The Earned Life*, he worked with CEOs at the pinnacles of their careers—leaders running billion-dollar companies and making major impacts in their industries. But many of them shared a painful realization: They had reached the highest levels of professional success, yet their personal lives felt empty. Some were estranged from their children. Others had lost touch with longtime friends. They had allowed work to consume every corner of their lives, leaving little room for meaningful personal connection.

And the overwhelming consensus? They wished they had blocked more time in their calendars for the people who mattered most to them.

That's the disconnect. We say relationships are a priority, but if they aren't in our calendar, they're not really a priority.

One of the first things I often tell leaders is, "Show me your calendar, and I'll show you your priorities." Usually, when I say this, they squirm a little bit. They're afraid to show me their calendars because they already know—their calendars *don't* reflect their priorities, and they need to make a change.

Show me your calendar, and I'll show you your priorities.

What would your response be if I asked you to show me your calendar? Would it reflect what—or *who*—matters most to you?

We all tend to fill our calendars reactively—with meetings, deadlines, and obligations—leaving little room for the people who actually matter most. We tell ourselves we'll find time later, but later never comes unless we intentionally make it.

That's where a *connection cadence* comes in—a consistent rhythm of reaching out, checking in, and showing up for the people who matter.

Think of a connection cadence like watering your plants. If you do it inconsistently—underwatering one week, forgetting the next, then overwatering the third—they'll struggle to thrive. I learned all about this when I hired a local landscaper to create a botanical installation in my home. Yes, you heard that right—a botanical installation. I'm semiobsessed with plants. There are at least six in every room.

So when Luna Botanicals showed up with what felt like an entire jungle, I had to get serious—because inconsistent watering, an *inconsistent cadence*, would have been a death sentence for these lush, vibrant plants. So I set a routine: Every Sunday, I walk through my house with my watering can, giving each plant the care it needs. Same time, same amount, every week. That's what keeps them not just alive but thriving.

Relationships work the same way. Without a steady cadence—a predictable pattern of care—they wither. But with regular, intentional effort, they flourish.

And just like in business—where companies use connection cadences to meet with their people, nurture leads, retain clients, and maintain networks—you need one in your own life to sustain the relationships that truly matter.

It's lonely at the top.

50%

of leaders struggle with loneliness

61%

of them believe it hurts their performance*

* "The Silent Struggle of CEOs: Why Leadership Can Be Lonely," Lakeside HR Group, https://lakesidehrgroup.com/2024/08/the-silent-struggle-of-ceos-why-leadership-can-be-lonely.

Gone are the days when you had a work calendar and a personal calendar. You have *one* life, *one* calendar (remember—work–life integration). Shifting your calendar means working backward—embedding time with the people who matter first, before the rest of your schedule fills up with obligations.

Because if you don't, you risk becoming the high-achieving leader who wakes up one day to realize success came at the cost of meaningful connection with the people you value the most in your life.

So, let's talk about how to shift your calendar—not just to manage your time but to align it with what (and who) matters most to YOU.

Make Your Calendar Match Your Priorities

My work with Taylor Johnson didn't stop at the *Best of Me* exercise. Once I mapped out what fuels me and identified my top priorities, Taylor hit me with another challenge:

"If someone looked at your calendar, would they see your actual priorities—or just a list of obligations?"

At first glance, my schedule looked impressive. Full. Productive. Packed with meetings, speaking engagements, workshops, and coaching calls. But when I stepped back, I saw the problem.

It was all work.

When my first book, *The Seismic Shift in Leadership*, became a bestseller, my mission became crystal clear: I wanted to help leaders connect better. So I poured everything into it—going on a book tour, launching *The Seismic Shift* podcast, giving speeches, and creating leadership academies—all with the goal of helping as many people as possible.

But in the process, I was putting work first. And while I love working on my mission, I couldn't ignore what was missing from my calendar: time with the friends who ground me, the relationships that make me feel fully seen, the people who lift me up and remind me who I am outside of my job.

In my effort to help everyone else connect, I was feeling completely disconnected myself.

Talk about irony.

I had always said relationships were my top priority. But my calendar told a different story.

> **I had always said relationships were my top priority. But my calendar told a different story.**

So Taylor and I dove into my calendar. We started with my most meaningful connections. *Who keeps me grounded? Who challenges me, encourages me, and reminds me of what matters? And most importantly—where are they in my schedule?*

This wasn't just about adding more time with friends and family. It was about shifting my entire approach to time. Instead of squeezing in connection when I could, I needed to prioritize it and carve out time for it. Because if I didn't, everything else would fill in the space.

During a conversation on my podcast, Taylor shared how he and his partner prioritize connection. It's an excellent example of a connection cadence—a rhythm designed to ensure the most important relationships don't get lost in the noise of daily life.

- Annually, they take a trip—to reflect, set goals, and align on their vision for the future.
- Quarterly, they carve out a long weekend together.
- Monthly, they plan a day trip—something simple but intentional like a hike.
- Weekly, they protect a meal together.
- Daily, no matter what, they check in with three questions:
- *Is there anything we need to clear up?*
- *What are we grateful for?*
- *What was your favorite moment today?*

Isn't this amazing? Not complicated. Not time-consuming. Just *intentional.*

And that was the word that stuck with me: *intentional.*

I was great at fitting in time with people when I could. A quick call here, a coffee date when schedules aligned, a text when I thought of someone. But real connection—the kind that builds trust, depth, and longevity—needs more than that. Real connection has to be woven into the rhythm of our lives.

Taylor's words hit me: "If you don't assign your time a purpose, it will be taken over by whatever is loudest and most urgent."

I had been waiting for time to open up. Instead, I needed to schedule the time—and protect it.

In the same way Taylor establishes his connection cadence with his partner, he encourages his clients to think about connection in layers:

- **ANNUALLY:** What relationships do you want to nurture over the course of a year? What commitments will help keep those connections strong?
- **QUARTERLY:** Who do you want to check in with on a deeper level? How can you create a rhythm that ensures those relationships don't fade into the background?
- **MONTHLY:** Which connections need regular attention? What recurring touchpoints will help maintain them?
- **WEEKLY AND DAILY:** How can you build a consistent, intentional cadence with the people you value most?

Find the Rituals That Connect You

Speaking of rhythms, one of the reasons I fell madly in love with New Orleans was the rhythm of connection that pulses through the city. This place is built on rituals—traditions that bring people together over and over again. And nowhere is that more obvious than Mardi Gras.

As I write this, the city is buzzing with marching bands warming up in the distance and the unmistakable hum of a Mardi Gras parade fills the air. If you've never been to Mardi Gras, let me tell you—it's an entire season of celebration, stretching from early January until the actual day of Mardi Gras—Fat Tuesday—which shifts dates each year based on the Easter calendar.

What makes this season especially magical to me is the way the community connects in the most creative ways.

Have you always wanted to dance in a parade? Want to be part of a float? There's a krewe for that. Age, gender, background—it doesn't matter. If you're willing to show up, practice, and have fun, you can learn the routines and march through the city, decked out in sequins and bursting with joy. And—best of all—your year is suddenly filled with float dinners, dance rehearsals, planning meetings, and decorating sessions. The fun starts long before parade day.

Sure, there are parts of Mardi Gras that remain closed or invitation-only—but over the last twenty years, the celebration has opened wide to welcome new ways of participating, inviting more people into the joy, creativity, and connection that make it so special.

When I joined Muses, one of the all-female parade krewes, I found myself immersed in a year-long rhythm of connection. We gathered to decorate shoes, met for float luncheons, and celebrated together at every stage of preparation. The community, the traditions, the shared anticipation—it became part of my calendar, part of my life.

Mardi Gras taught me that connection has to be built with intention. These traditions exist because people commit to them. They make time. They show up. They build these moments into the rhythm of their lives.

And that's what I want you to take from this. Maybe you're reading this thinking, *Well, I don't live in New Orleans, Michelle.* But there are opportunities everywhere—if you're willing to look for them. Maybe it's a local running club that meets every Saturday, a community theater group that puts on productions each season, or a volunteer organization that gathers regularly to make an impact. It could be a neighborhood softball league, a choir, or a group that hosts monthly potlucks.

The key is to find something that brings people together on a regular basis—a shared experience that creates connection, rhythm, and a sense of belonging.

Marshall on Shifting Your Calendar

Michelle said it best: "Show me your calendar, and I'll show you your priorities." Your calendar tells the truth. But the truth isn't always easy to face.

In leadership—and in life—it's one thing to intend to make space for what matters. It's another to actually do it. We tell ourselves the right stories:

"I value my family."

"My people are my priority."

"Relationships come first."

But until those values show up on the calendar—not just as blocked time but as real presence—they're just words.

I've seen it play out with leaders around the world. Let me tell you a story about Fred Lynch, a former client who became a friend. Fred once shared something with me that brought this lesson home.

Fred was the president and CEO of Masonite International—a high-demand, high-pressure role. He was constantly busy, juggling decisions, meetings, and responsibilities. But during the years when his kids were teenagers, Fred made a conscious decision: He wanted to be more present with his family. He envisioned connection—dinners where they'd share about their day, laugh, and stay close despite the busyness of life. So he made a rule: Everyone home for dinner, every night.

At first, his kids resisted. Teenagers aren't usually thrilled about family mandates, especially ones that cut into their independence. But eventually, they adapted. Dinner became a routine. Fred was doing it—family dinners, just like he imagined.

But one evening, as they sat around the table in silence, Fred was absorbed in his phone, checking work emails between bites.

His daughter looked at him and said what everyone else was thinking:

"You wanted us to be here for family dinner, but you're always on your phone. What's the point?"

That moment hit him hard. He had made the plan. He had set the expectation. But he wasn't showing up fully. The intention was there, but the action wasn't aligned.

This is what happens when we treat connection like a calendar event—something we show up for physically but not emotionally. We confuse showing up with being present.

In leadership, I often encourage people to engage in stakeholder coaching—a process that starts with asking the most important people in your life, "How can I be better?" It's a powerful question. Most people say they believe in listening to feedback. Most say they care about relationships. But when I ask leaders if they've ever asked their spouse or children a question like this, I'm often met with silence.

I started asking my kids that question when my daughter Kelly was eleven and my son Bryan was nine. "What can I do to be a better father?"

The challenge with asking that question is—you get an answer.

Kelly said, "Daddy, you travel a lot. That's not what bothers me. What bothers me is the way you act when you come home. You talk on the phone. You watch sports. You don't spend much time with me."

Then she told me something I'll never forget: "One time, I had to stay home from a party to spend time with you, and then you didn't spend time with me. That wasn't right."

She was right. I had to own that.

I promised to do better. I started tracking how many days I could spend at least four hours with my family. In 1991, it was 92 days. Then 110. Then 131. By 1994, it was 135 days.

Interestingly, I made more money that year than in years when I'd barely seen my family. I also learned a critical truth: The San Diego Chargers don't care about me. And, as it turns out, they don't even care about San Diego—they moved to L.A.

Then came January 1, 1995. I was feeling proud. I had my tracking charts in hand and presented them to my now-teenage kids. "Look! 135

days with Dad! What should our goal be this year? How about 150?"

Both of them said, "No, Daddy. You have overachieved."

Bryan added, "I think 50 is a better number to go for."

They voted for a massive cutback in Dad-time. Turns out, we were all growing up.

Even though my kids weren't interested in spending 150 days with me, my intention was clear. I wanted my words and my actions to clearly align. Because here's what I've learned, both in my own life and in my work with leaders around the world: We often confuse saying something is important with showing that it is. We think intention equals impact. But if we don't follow through—if we don't make real space for it—it's just talk.

Saying your family is important doesn't make it true. Making time to be fully present at dinner—without the phone—does.

Saying you want to be a better parent doesn't move the needle. Listening to your child's feedback—and adjusting your behavior—does.

We can't just articulate our priorities. We have to live them. And one of the clearest ways to do that is through your calendar.

Because here's the truth: Your calendar isn't just a schedule. It's a mirror. It reflects where you're showing up—and where you're not.

Shifting your calendar is about making the invisible visible. It's about turning good intentions into meaningful, consistent action.

How to Build a Connection Cadence

Building meaningful connection doesn't happen by accident. It takes reflection, intention, and a little trial and error. One of the simplest ways to anchor connection in your life is by focusing on the "Three Rs" we've discussed in this chapter: relationships, rituals, and rhythms—in other words, who, what, and how often.

Here's how to put them into practice:

1 WHO? PRIORITIZE THE RELATIONSHIPS THAT MATTER MOST

Start by naming the people who ground, challenge, and support you—both personally and professionally. Who do you want to intentionally invest in? Write down their names and reflect on what these relationships need to stay strong.

2 WHAT? CREATE RITUALS THAT BRING YOU TOGETHER

Don't wait for the perfect time to invest in the people who matter most. Put it on the calendar now. Maybe it's a monthly book club, a community sports league, or a volunteer group that gathers regularly to serve. These rituals—meaningful, repeated events—create shared experience and deepen connection over time. Start by choosing one relationship or group you want to be more intentional about this season. What's one way you can create space for that connection? If you don't have a ritual like this, look for one. And if you can't find one, start one.

3 WHEN? ESTABLISH RHYTHMS THAT SUSTAIN CONNECTION

Start big: Decide when to have your annual retreat, family vacation, or reunion with old friends. Then layer in quarterly and monthly rhythms—steady check-ins like a mentor lunch or dinner with close friends. Finally, protect the weekly and daily events that keep you present: a date night, a walk with a friend, or a daily check-in. These consistent patterns—the *rhythm*—become the heartbeat of connection in your everyday life.

As life shifts, your relationships, rituals, and rhythms will shift too. That's okay. The goal is to create a cadence that adapts with you. If something isn't working, tweak it. If a connection needs more (or less), adjust. The key is to stay intentional and keep prioritizing the people who matter most.

YOUR CHALLENGE

Make a Seismic Shift in Your Calendar

Take a hard look at your schedule. Does it reflect your most important relationships? Is there a steady cadence? If not, make one change. Maybe it's scheduling that overdue coffee date with a friend, blocking time for a one-on-one check-in with a colleague you rarely see anymore, or setting a recurring dinner date with your family. Start small, but start now. Because the connections that matter most deserve more than the crumbs of your leftover time.

SHIFT YOUR MEETINGS

Do your meetings encourage dialogue?

Transform your meetings into ones that are engaging and interactive. YOUR people will thank you.

CHAPTER FOUR

SHIFT YOUR MEETINGS

"The majority of meetings should be discussions that lead to decisions."

—PATRICK LENCIONI

"The success of a meeting depends on each individual making a contribution."

—UNKNOWN

We've all been in meetings that seem to drain the life out of us—stiff, top-down sessions where the stakes feel high but the outcomes fall short. Instead of fostering connection and collaboration, they leave us feeling isolated, uninspired, and frustrated—because, let's face it, they often feel like a waste of time.

I've seen this dynamic play out across the globe. Omar was a finance leader who ran his team meetings more like interrogation rooms than collaborative spaces. He had an uncanny knack for spotting the smallest errors—especially in spreadsheets—and calling people out with a condescending tone in front of the entire team.

Each month, the team gathered—not to collaborate or solve problems but to defend themselves. Team members would arrive in their most formal attire, PowerPoint slides polished to perfection, bracing themselves for scrutiny. The meetings weren't about growth or teamwork or even outcomes; they were about *control*. Omar's control.

Team members said they spent the week before these meetings on edge, not sleeping, overeating, triple-checking everything just to avoid being "caught." Instead of collaborating as a team, they were competitive with each other, defensive, and emotionally drained. Eventually, the climate of fear reached its breaking point. HR stepped in. The feedback was blunt: This hostile meeting culture was destroying motivation and mental health.

When you're stuck in a place of fear like this, productivity takes a nosedive and innovation disappears. In the end, Omar's approach didn't just hurt his team—he lost his job.

The Seismic Shift in Meetings

In contrast, Pete November, CEO of Ochsner Health—the largest employer in Louisiana—approaches meetings with connection as the ultimate priority. Long before becoming CEO, Pete understood that a team needs more than a shared agenda to succeed—it needs a sense of unity.

So, when he inherited a team made up of disconnected divisions, Pete crafted intentional moments of connection to bring the team together, even though they didn't interact daily.

He began every meeting with a personal and professional check-in, often asking team members to share recognition for someone in or outside of the room or give kudos to a special project that team members were proud of that week. At first people were hesitant, but soon people were coming together to celebrate everyone's good news.

Pete had a bigger goal in mind: He wanted the entire team to know and understand each other—not just through their work but through their stories. The impact of appreciation and gratitude was immediate.

Relationships were built in an environment of understanding and collaboration. As a result, people could work together cohesively in meetings because they felt comfortable sharing and also because many were receiving valued recognition for their work in an open forum.

One meeting, right before Thanksgiving, Pete asked the group to share their favorite Thanksgiving dish. It seemed simple enough, but what followed was one of those magical connection moments. Team members swapped family traditions, shared recipes, and even told stories about loved ones. By the end of the meeting (a virtual meeting, at that), there was a tangible shift in energy—a feeling of unity inspired by a deeper understanding of each other.

That trust was tested during a health crisis that required cross-functional collaboration. Because Pete had invested in connection, the team was able to rally, working seamlessly across departments. They launched new initiatives, including developing a product supply line to meet critical needs—something that wouldn't have been possible without the trust and cohesion Pete had built. Those early moments of connecting became the foundation for resilience, creativity, and genuine teamwork.

Even when meetings were only once a month for an hour and a half, Pete spent up to thirty minutes building connection. Why? Because he knew that understanding each other as humans—not just coworkers—was the foundation for any successful team.

The contrast is stark: Fear-driven meetings breed isolation and burnout, while connection-focused meetings empower teams to face challenges together.

The contrast is stark: Fear-driven meetings breed isolation and burnout, while connection-focused meetings empower teams to face challenges together.

Some leaders may feel they don't have time to prioritize connection, but the truth is, without it, productivity, engagement, and innovation suffer.

71%

Managers who consider meetings to be inefficient

$37 billion

The loss as a result of unproductive meetings*

---

* Ron Carucci, "How to Fix the Most Soul-Crushing Meetings," *Harvard Business Review*, https://hbr.org/2018/02/how-to-fix-the-most-soul-crushing-meetings.

In a world where workplace connection is increasingly rare, leaders can't afford to overlook it. Teams thrive when they know each other's stories, trust each other, and feel supported. Shifting meetings from rigid control to authentic connection creates an environment where people feel seen, heard, and motivated to bring their best.

Shift Your Agenda

Think about the last meeting you attended. Did you feel engaged, like your presence truly mattered? Or did you find yourself wondering, *Why am I here? What's the point of this?*

We've all sat through meetings that felt like a waste of time. But what if meetings aren't the problem? What if the real issue is how they're run?

This is where Dr. Steven Rogelberg's work shines. When I interviewed him on my podcast, it was easy to see why he's the go-to expert on meetings. As an organizational psychologist, a chancellor professor at UNC Charlotte, and the author of *Glad We Met: The Art and Science of 1:1 Meetings*, Steven has spent his career helping leaders turn meetings into spaces for real collaboration.

One of his biggest insights is that meetings themselves aren't the enemy—it's just the bad ones that need to go. And one of the most practical yet powerful shifts is leading with agenda *questions* instead of agenda *items*.

Instead of "project updates," imagine starting your next meeting with a question: "*What decisions do we need to make today?*" That small change shifts a meeting from a passive update to an active conversation where people engage, contribute, and problem-solve together.

Instead of "project updates," imagine starting your next meeting with a question: "*What decisions do we need to make today?*"

I've experienced this kind of connection-driven meeting firsthand as part of the 100 Coaches group. After working with some of the top executives in the world, Marshall saw how isolating leadership can be. So, he created a group of CEOs, consultants, and coaches who could come together to listen, learn, and above all, connect.

Every meeting starts with clarity. Bill Carrier, the president of 100 Coaches, opens our bimonthly Zoom meetings by setting the tone with a clear statement: "The mission of 100 Coaches is to elevate individual world-class leaders through connection and learning." That reminder frames everything that follows.

Then, Marshall sets the stage with a thought-provoking topic, sharing insights from his own experience and inviting us into the conversation. From there, we jump into breakout rooms—smaller groups where we exchange perspectives, learn from each other, and engage in real discussion. In a virtual setting, these breakout rooms are essential for creating meaningful connection and giving everyone a chance to contribute. We're not just talked at; we're part of it.

By the time we return to the main session, the energy is electric. Ideas are flowing, new connections are forming, and people leave with insights they can actually use. And that's the difference. I don't just walk away with information—I walk away with a sense of belonging.

This is what great meetings do. They create space for engagement, connection, and real impact. When meetings are designed with intention, people feel valued and invested. And that changes everything.

Deepen Connection Through Movement

Connection-driven meetings inspire dialogue, but Bart Foster takes it further—challenging us to rethink not just how we meet but where and why. As the founder of BusinessOutside and author of the book by the same name, Bart has redefined what it means to connect. He's all about ditching the tired, traditional approach to meetings and instead embracing something more dynamic and creative.

I got to experience this firsthand at a leadership retreat he hosted in Austin, Texas. I was invited as the keynote speaker for a group of CEOs, and my plan was straightforward: Fly in, deliver my talk, and fly out. But Bart had a different idea.

"Why don't you stay for the full two and a half days?" he asked. "Experience what we do." So, I did. And I'm so glad I stuck around.

The retreat kicked off with my keynote speech on connection, where I shared my research and led the group through my Connection Catalyst Assessment (CCA). This tool helps people identify their dominant connection style—whether they naturally prioritize relationships, results, information, or efficiency when they're interacting with others. (It's something I use often with my clients to improve team communication—and if you're curious, you can take it yourself at michellekjohnston.com/assessment.)

That evening, Bart hosted a Jeffersonian dinner where each person at the table opened an envelope with three carefully crafted questions. One by one, we took turns answering. I expected surface-level business chatter, but what unfolded was something else entirely.

Within minutes, these CEOs were sharing deeply personal stories of struggle—addiction, miscarriages, divorces, bankruptcies. There was no small talk, no posturing. Just honesty, vulnerability, and real human connection. Somehow, the structure of the evening—the thoughtful questions, the intentional space for everyone to speak—created a depth of conversation most meetings never reach.

The next morning, we traded conference chairs for a 3.5-mile "connection walk" along the Colorado River. As we walked side by side, conversations flowed naturally. Bart calls it "motion creating emotion," and he's right. There's something about movement that makes people open up. By the time we reached our destination—an innovation center for talks with visionary entrepreneurs—we weren't just a group of CEOs. We were a connected community.

That evening, instead of the usual networking dinner with a keynote at a podium, we sat fireside for an intimate Q&A with Carla Piñeyro

Sublett, former CMO at IBM and an inspiring entrepreneur. The next morning, at a connection breakfast, we reflected on what we'd learned, sharing insights and takeaways.

As I reflected on the flight home, I was struck by how every moment of the retreat had been intentionally designed to foster connection.

Bart doesn't just talk about connection—he lives it. And having walked alongside him—both literally and figuratively—I can tell you his approach is transformational. Meetings don't have to feel like soul-draining slogs in a windowless room. They can actually be creative, energizing, and maybe even a little fun.

Meetings don't have to feel like soul-draining slogs in a windowless room. They can actually be creative, energizing, and maybe even a little fun.

Whether it's a walk, a dinner, a picnic, or a hike, real connection happens when we create space for deeper conversations and when we show up ready to engage.

Marshall on Shifting Your Meetings

Michelle is right—meetings have a bad reputation. They're often dreaded, endured, and then forgotten. But she's also right that meetings don't have to be energy-draining. In fact, they can become some of the most engaging, empowering, and energizing moments of your day—if you approach them with intention.

Shifting your meetings is one of the most practical ways to change how your organization feels, how people interact, and how work gets done.

One of the most powerful ways to do this is by applying a basic tool I teach called the "Did I do my best to . . . ?" questions. The twist is that you ask them *before* the meeting—not as a reflection on what happened, but as a way to set your intention.

Before walking into any meeting—especially one you're dreading—imagine that *afterward*, you'll be evaluated based on these questions:

- *Did I do my best to be fully engaged?*
- *Did I do my best to build positive relationships?*
- *Did I do my best to find meaning?*
- *Did I do my best to be happy?*

Think about a routine update or a slide-heavy presentation—the kind of meeting where it's easy to disengage or mentally check out. Now imagine this: At the end of that meeting, the focus won't be on the presenter or the content. It will be on you. How well did *you* show up? How well did *you* live out those four questions?

Suddenly, the meeting feels different. Maybe you'd prepare a little more. Maybe you'd offer support, ask a thoughtful question, connect with someone new. You'd tune in instead of tuning out.

I've seen this reframe unlock surprising engagement. People start saying things like, "I'll bring donuts." "I'll actually listen." "I'll try to help." Small actions—but transformative ones that foster connection.

One striking example of this kind of shift comes from Alan Mulally, who became CEO of Ford in 2006 when the company was in crisis. It had just posted the largest loss in its 103-year history. Stock had dropped to $1 per share. Employees were demoralized, anxious, and unsure about the company's future.

Alan didn't walk in with grand speeches or blame. He didn't start barking orders or scrambling to cut costs. Instead, he changed the way their meetings worked before he arrived.

He introduced a weekly ritual called the Business Plan Review—or BPR. Every week, Alan and his sixteen executives would review their areas of the business and report progress using a color-coded system:

- GREEN: On track, no issues.
- YELLOW: Some challenges, with a clear plan for resolution.
- RED: Not on track, and working together on a plan to get back on track.

At the very first BPR, all sixteen leaders reported GREEN. Alan looked around the room—calmly and kindly—and said, "If everything is green and we are forecasting a yearly loss of $17 billion, wouldn't it be valuable to share the issues that are causing our forecasted loss so we can work on them together? Let's try this next week."

For the next few weeks, nothing changed, as the team members were concerned—because of their history before Alan arrived—about not having a psychologically safe culture for sharing issues. Then Mark Fields (who would later become Ford's CEO) finally raised his hand and said, "Red." He named a major issue, as Alan had requested.

Alan didn't flinch. He didn't critique. He didn't jump in with a fix.

He stood up and applauded.

"Mark, thank you," he said. "That's exactly what we need—timely transparency. And to be clear, I don't have the answer either. But we have a room full of intelligent and highly motivated people here. We can figure it out working together."

That single moment shifted Ford's meeting culture to one of psychological safety—from fear to trust and from isolation to connection and collaboration. Alan's approach showed his team it's okay to admit problems, it's okay to ask for help, and it's okay to work through uncertainty by working together.

This "working together" cultural shift was one of the key foundations of Ford's legendary turnaround—becoming the number one automotive brand in the United States and the fastest-growing automotive brand in the world.

How to Run a Connection-Driven Meeting

What if your meetings weren't just another obligation on the calendar—but something your team actually looked forward to? What if they created spaces where ideas sparked, connections deepened, and real progress happened? With a few intentional shifts, meetings can be engaging, dynamic, and even inspiring.

So, how do we get there?

1 RETHINK YOUR ROLE

As a leader, you cultivate the environment where people feel safe to speak up, ask questions, and share ideas. That starts with showing up with curiosity, really listening, and staying open to different perspectives. Before you walk in, ask yourself: *How do I want to show up? What kind of experience do I want to create?*

2 BEGIN WITH CONNECTION

Before diving into the agenda, take a moment to check in. A quick question—"What's one win from this week?" or "How are you feeling on a scale from one to ten?"—sets the tone for trust and camaraderie. Even in remote meetings, breakout rooms can create space for smaller, more meaningful conversations. A little connection up-front makes everything that follows more engaging.

3 LEAD WITH QUESTIONS

Instead of running through a list of updates, try shifting the focus. *What decisions do we need to make today? What's standing in our way?* Framing meetings around thoughtful questions turns them into active problem-solving sessions instead of passive information dumps. It invites engagement and sparks real discussion.

4 GET PEOPLE MOVING

A change in physical space can completely transform the energy in a meeting. Take a page from Bart's playbook and try a "connection walk" outside or encourage people to stand instead of sitting the whole time. Movement opens up creativity and conversation in ways a conference table just can't.

5 **DESIGN THE EXPERIENCE**

Meetings don't have to follow a formula. Try a Jeffersonian-style discussion. Rotate through "team storytellers"—people who kick off the meeting with a quick story that reflects your organization's values, highlights a recent win, or sparks reflection. Build in moments of reflection or celebration. Treat each meeting like it matters and show up with presence, intention, and the energy you want others to feel.

6 **MODEL OPENNESS**

What if you approached your next meeting the way Alan Mulally did when he stepped in as Ford's CEO? Invite your team to share where they have challenges in implementing their plans. Work through the challenges together. Celebrate transparency and working together. Create a culture where people feel safe to share their real challenges, offer real help, and build real trust.

With a few intentional changes, you can create meetings where trust builds, ideas flow, and real progress happens. Imagine the impact if every meeting felt like an opportunity to connect—imagine the joy, the purpose, and the energy that would flow out of that.

YOUR CHALLENGE

Make a Seismic Shift in Your Meetings

It's time to shake things up. Choose one meeting and do it differently. Skip the PowerPoint. Try a connection walk. Take it outside or just reframe the conversation or agenda with creative, pointed questions. Make connection the ultimate goal—because when your team feels connected, ideas flow more freely, engagement goes up, and the results speak for themselves.

SHIFT YOUR CONVERSATIONS

Do you talk more than listen?

Talking at someone is not going to get YOU what you want. Connection is more than what you say, it's how the other person feels.

CHAPTER FIVE
SHIFT YOUR CONVERSATIONS

"Poor communication reduces trust both in leadership and in their team for over 40 percent of workers."*

—LEERON HOORY

Okay, y'all, I'm going to be really honest with you.

When I began writing this book with Marshall, I was beyond excited. I took a sabbatical from my faculty responsibilities at Loyola, and I was ready to dive in. My number one priority was to get the book written before heading back to teaching in the fall.

I felt confident we'd find a natural rhythm. Our relationship was already strong—our conversations flowed easily, and I deeply admired Marshall's brilliance, generosity, and sense of humor. I was so excited to get started, I just charged ahead, assuming the approach that had worked for my first book would work here too. It didn't even cross my mind to pause and have a conversation about process.

I scheduled brainstorming Zooms and planning calls, eager to keep

* Leeron Hoory, "The State Of Workplace Communication," *Forbes,* March 8, 2023, https://www.forbes.com/advisor/business/digital-communication-workplace.

things moving. Coordinating schedules was really difficult, but I kept pushing forward, assuming we'd eventually settle into a good rhythm.

A few months in, I happened to interview Michael Bungay Stanier (MBS), best-selling author of *The Coaching Habit*, on my podcast. As we talked, he introduced me to his concept of the "keystone conversation"—a conversation to lay the foundation for how you'll work together. With over 1.5 million copies of his book sold—and self-published, no less—MBS knows a thing or two about setting the stage for success.

Listening to MBS, the lightbulb didn't just go off—it exploded. I realized I had completely skipped one of the most important steps in any collaboration: sitting down and having a real conversation about how we were going to work together.

I realized I'd completely skipped one of the most important steps in any collaboration: sitting down and having a real conversation about how we were going to work together.

Thankfully (*thanks to MBS*), I caught this insight early enough in the book process to course-correct. I sat down with Marshall, and together we had the keystone conversation we should have started with, asking crucial questions of one another: *What does successful collaboration look like? What's worked for you in the past? What's the best way for us to approach this book-writing process?*

And from that moment on, everything became easier, smoother, and more energizing. We found a rhythm that honored what worked best for both of us, and the project came to life in a way we're incredibly proud of.

So yes—I wish I'd initiated that first keystone conversation from the start. But the good news is, it's never too late. Once we had that conversation, it made all the difference. And the even better news? You're holding the result of that great collaboration in your hands.

The Seismic Shift in Conversations

Think about the last conversation you had. How did you feel afterward? Did you feel heard, valued, and understood—or dismissed and discouraged? *Why?*

Now let's flip the question—how do you think people feel after talking with you? How do you think your *teams* feel after talking with you? Do they leave feeling empowered and engaged, or do they walk away feeling like their voices don't matter?

Marshall has a saying I love: "Successful people become great leaders when they learn to shift the focus from themselves to others." That shift in attention changes everything. Because impactful leadership involves far more than managing tasks or ticking boxes—it's about building relationships. And relationships are built through meaningful conversations.

Unfortunately, too many workplaces fall into the trap of top-down communication. You've seen it, right? Performance reviews that feel like one-way critiques, directives handed down without input, and one-on-ones that seem to drain more energy than they generate. And somewhere along the way, the humanity of the team gets lost in the grind of productivity.

Thankfully, there's a better way. Meaningful conversations go beyond exchanging information—they're about encouraging *dialogue*, building understanding, and solving problems together. By asking thoughtful questions, listening with genuine curiosity, and leaning into moments of vulnerability, you can foster an environment where people leave conversations feeling valued, heard, and engaged.

By asking thoughtful questions, listening with genuine curiosity, and leaning into moments of vulnerability, you can foster an environment where people leave conversations feeling valued, heard, and engaged.

This is the heart of the seismic shift in conversations. It's about moving from speaking *at* people to truly engaging *with* them. It's replacing critique with coaching and shifting from talking to actively listening. When your conversations are grounded in curiosity and empathy, you build a culture where trust flourishes, voices are heard, and success becomes a collective journey.

Here's the best part—it's not just your team that benefits. The ripple effects of meaningful conversations will deepen your own sense of purpose and confidence. Watching the impact of your leadership unfold through genuine connection can be one of the most rewarding parts of the journey.

So, how do you start leaning into those conversations that matter? It begins with asking the right questions.

The Power of Great Questions

One of the most valuable lessons I've learned from Marshall is that leadership isn't about having all the answers. It's about asking the kinds of questions that help others uncover their own answers. Marshall is a master at this—he's constantly asking open-ended questions like, "What's your perspective on this challenge?" or "What do you think is the best path forward?" It's why he's such a successful coach—his approach empowers people to think critically and take ownership.

Leadership isn't about having all the answers. It's about asking the kinds of questions that help others uncover their own answers.

MBS's keystone conversation—which he unpacks in his best-selling book *How to Work with (Almost) Anyone*—applies this approach of asking open-ended questions to pivotal moments. These include times when someone joins a team, when dynamics shift, or when tackling a major project. Have a conversation where each of you answer the following five questions:

1. *What's your best?*
2. *What are your practices and preferences?*
3. *What can we learn from successful past relationships?*
4. *What can we learn from frustrating past relationships?*
5. *How will we fix it when things go wrong?*

What I love most about these questions is how they create space for genuine connection. They're all about understanding the person in front of you. And when you share your own answers in return, you lay the foundation for a partnership built on mutual trust, understanding, and respect. That's the kind of alignment we all hope for before starting something new!

The Power of Empathy

Of course, asking the right questions is only part of the equation. To have truly impactful conversations, you also need to show empathy. No one understood this better than my dear, late friend Dr. Mark Goulston, a renowned author and psychiatrist. Mark was one of those rare people who made you feel completely seen and heard every time you spoke with him. He had this extraordinary ability to create a safe space where you could open up, and he taught me so much about the art of connection.

Mark introduced me to the concept of "surgical empathy," which goes beyond surface-level conversation. It's about tuning in so deeply that you help people uncover what they're feeling but might not yet have the words to express. It takes effort, but this kind of listening is transformative—it's a powerful tool to deepen your impact and leave people feeling truly seen and heard.

Mark's "Five Reallys" are a tool I find myself using all the time. They're great for those moments when someone gives you the classic "I'm fine" answer. You follow up with, "But really, how's it going?" and then gently ask again, "Really, how's it going?" You keep going—naturally, of course—until they feel comfortable enough to open up (usually around five times, hence the name). Taking the time to go deeper and explore the "really" demonstrates care, compassion, and true empathy.

And yes, sometimes what they share might be heavy. If it is, Mark has said it's okay to set boundaries. If you're not in a position to give them your full attention after hearing about their situation, you can say, "This topic is too important to rush. Let's set a time when we can really talk."

Mark also believed that having meaningful conversations is just the start—we also need to consider how those conversations might have landed with the other person. Of course, we can't really know how they feel unless we ask, but his H.U.V.A. framework is a great way to reflect on whether we're creating a positive experience:

- **H: HEARD:** Did the person feel truly listened to, without interruption?
- **U: UNDERSTOOD:** Did you show you understood their emotions by asking thoughtful follow-up questions?
- **V: VALUED:** Did you acknowledge something unique or impressive about what they shared?
- **A: ADDED VALUE:** Did you leave them with something meaningful, like encouragement or insight?

Having meaningful conversations is just the start—we also need to consider how those conversations might have landed with the other person.

It's a reminder that the success of a conversation depends on how the other person feels after it. And it's not about being perfect; as Mark used to say, it's about making progress. Each time we listen with intention and empathy, we strengthen the connection—and those connections change lives.

Leaning into Delicate Conversations

Even with great question-asking and active listening, we all have those conversations we'd rather avoid, don't we? Whether it's giving feedback, addressing a promotion request, or delivering tough news, these moments can feel like walking a tightrope. That's where Alisa Cohn shines. Recognized as the number one startup coach in the world, Alisa has guided leaders through some of the most challenging conversations they'll ever face—and she does it in a way that's refreshingly straightforward.

Alisa doesn't call these difficult conversations; she calls them *delicate*—and there's a reason for that. Think about it: When we label something as difficult, we brace for conflict. Or expect tension. That framing can turn the conversation into something to fear or avoid. (More on the power of language in the next chapter!)

But when we label something as *delicate*—like a package marked *fragile*—we instinctively handle it with more care. We slow down. We approach it with intention and respect. What if we brought that perspective into these kinds of conversations? When we view them as delicate rather than difficult, they can become something more—an opportunity to build trust and create deeper connection with the people we're talking to.

What if we view these conversations as delicate rather than difficult? Then they can become something more—an opportunity to build trust and create deeper connections with the people we're talking to.

Take, for instance, an employee asking for a promotion they're not quite ready for. Instead of delivering a flat no, Alisa suggests starting with recognition: "You've been such an important part of the team, and I'm grateful for the work you've done." From there, she encourages leaders to own any shortcomings in communication: "If I haven't been clear about the milestones for the next step, that's on me, and I want to fix that."

Then, shift the focus to collaboration: "Let's talk about what the next step looks like and how we can get you there." This approach turns what could be a tension-filled moment into a constructive conversation that shows your commitment to the other person's growth and future at the organization.

Or consider delivering hard news. Alisa's method starts with honesty: "I need to share some news. We didn't meet our revenue goals this quarter, and as a result, we're implementing a hiring freeze." Then, acknowledge the impact: "I know this isn't easy to hear, and I'm happy to answer any questions you have." Finally, offer a path forward: "We're already working on new strategies, and I believe we have the strength to move through this together."

Even with constructive feedback, Alisa's strategies transform potentially awkward conversations into connection opportunities. Let's say you're speaking with a team member who tends to dominate meetings. Instead of starting with criticism, lead with an honest strength: "Your enthusiasm and ideas bring so much energy to our discussions." Then, gently address the growth opportunity: "I've noticed that sometimes others don't get a chance to contribute. How can we work together to make sure everyone's voice is heard?"

What makes Alisa's advice so powerful is how approachable it feels. These conversations can be easier than you think. With a little preparation and the right mindset, you can make the most of these conversations to strengthen your team and build trust. If you're curious for more, Alisa's book, *From Start-Up to Grown-Up*, offers a treasure trove of scripts and insights for navigating delicate conversations with kindness and finesse.

Alisa often leaves leaders with a challenge, and I'll share it with you now: "*There's a conversation you're putting off, isn't there? Go have it. Plan it out, calm your nerves, and approach it with care. You'll feel better—and so will the other person.*"

Marshall on Shifting Your Conversations

All of this advice you've heard so far—from Michelle, MBS, Mark, and Alisa—points to a powerful truth: Connection is about more than what you say. It's about how you make people feel. Do they walk away from the conversation feeling respected? Heard? Valued?

For many leaders, the biggest obstacle to effective conversations isn't a lack of intelligence or strategy. It's the deep-seated habit of needing to win.

We've all done it. We push our ideas just a little too hard. We offer advice when none was asked for. We interrupt with a "better" version of someone else's point. We think we're helping, but in reality, we're undermining the connection we're trying to build.

I call this habit "winning too much"—the desire to win in all situations. To have the last word. To one-up someone's story. To improve someone's idea. To be right, even when being right isn't helpful.

Here's an example. You want to go to dinner at Restaurant X. Your partner wants to go to Restaurant Y. You argue but eventually go to Restaurant Y. The food is terrible. The service is worse. Now you have two options:

- Critique the food and remind your partner you were right.
- Say nothing and enjoy the evening together anyway.

What would most people do? Critique the food.

What should they do? Let it go.

Now imagine this dynamic at work. Someone offers a solid idea in a meeting. Instead of affirming it, you say, "Good idea—but it'd be even better if . . ."

In your mind, you've just improved the idea. In their mind, you've taken it.

That's the danger of adding "too much value." You may improve the idea by 5 percent—but you reduce the person's commitment to it by 50 percent. Because it's no longer theirs. It's yours.

The need to win doesn't just block connection—it shuts it down.

The higher up you go, the greater the risk. Because the more authority

96%

Employees who want a more empathetic approach to communication in the workplace*

* "20 Business & Workplace Communication Statistics [2024]," Simon & Simon, May 8, 2024, https://www.simonandsimon.co.uk/blog/20-business-workplace-communication-statistics.

you hold, the heavier your words land. What feels like a casual suggestion to you can feel like a mandate to the person on the receiving end.

Former GlaxoSmithKline CEO JP Garnier captured it perfectly: "My suggestions become orders. If they're smart, they're orders. If they're stupid, they're orders. If I want them to be orders, they're orders. And if I don't want them to be orders, they're orders anyway."

This is what makes the habit of winning so dangerous for leaders.

It doesn't just silence ideas—it silences people.

That's why one of the most powerful moves in leadership communication is also the simplest: *Talk less. Listen more.*

This isn't about being passive. It's about being intentional. It's knowing when your input builds connection—and when it shuts it down.

And it's not just about listening for the sake of courtesy. It's about showing people that their ideas matter. That *they* matter.

One of the easiest ways to do this is to start asking better questions. Instead of saying, "What do you think of my idea?" try "What's your perspective?" Not "Can I give you some advice?" but "How would you approach this?" And then—actually listen. No interrupting. No fixing. No improving.

This is where many leaders struggle. We confuse leadership with having answers. But great leadership isn't about dominating the dialogue. It's about creating space for others to contribute and grow.

If you don't make that space, people eventually stop showing up fully. They'll disengage—not because they don't care but because they don't feel heard.

In a coaching session, one young executive told me, "Every time I brought something to my boss, he'd tweak it or redirect it. Eventually, I thought, why bother? And I just stopped speaking up."

Contrast that with another leader who made a personal commitment to say less and listen more. She began every meeting with one question: "*What's something you've been thinking about that I might not know?*" That small shift changed everything. Her team started offering more ideas, identifying problems early, and bringing perspectives that would have otherwise gone unheard.

When leaders shift the conversation from performance to partnership, people lean in.

So the next time you feel the urge to prove your point, fix someone's idea, or have the last word, pause and ask yourself:

- *Is this really worth it?*
- *Am I trying to be helpful—or just trying to win?*
- *How will the other person feel after this conversation?*

Because the best leaders don't always have the best answers—they create space for others to find them. They don't just talk. They listen. They learn. And they lead in a way that makes others feel heard.

How to Engage in Meaningful Conversations

Meaningful conversations don't just happen. They require intentional questions, deep listening, and a willingness to engage the hard stuff. Are you taking the time to lean in with curiosity and care, or are you settling for surface-level exchanges out of habit or convenience?

Here are a few ways you can open the door to deeper connections through meaningful conversations:

1 START WITH CURIOSITY

Think about how your next conversation might feel if you approached it with curiosity. Questions like "What's your perspective on this?" or "What does success look like for you?" invite collaboration and signal that you value the other person's voice. As Marshall reminds us, sometimes the most powerful move you can make as a leader is to be quiet and simply listen.

2 LAY THE GROUNDWORK EARLY

Some of the best conversations happen before challenges arise. Taking time to align early—whether you're onboarding a new team member or starting a big project—can save a lot of confusion later. Consider questions like "What's the best way for us to work together?" or "What motivates you most in a role like this?" With MBS's keystone conversation, you can uncover strengths, preferences, and potential pain points ahead of time while building a foundation of trust.

3 SHOW EMPATHY

Empathy involves making the other person feel seen. Tools like Mark's "Five Reallys" remind us to gently go beyond surface-level exchanges: "How's it going? . . . But really, how's it going? . . . Really?" And as Marshall teaches, the higher up you go, the more your words weigh. People don't just hear your advice—they feel your influence. When you hold back from "adding value" and focus instead on being fully present, you send a clear signal to others: *Your voice matters here.*

4 TURN DELICATE CONVERSATIONS INTO CONNECTION OPPORTUNITIES

Addressing unmet expectations can feel daunting, but it doesn't have to be. In these conversations, start by acknowledging the other person's contributions: "Here's what I value about what you've done." Then state the opportunity for improvement. For example, "Here's an area we can work on together." This approach shifts the tone from criticism to collaboration, creating an opportunity to show your investment in the other person's growth.

5 APPROACH TOUGH TOPICS WITH CARE

When it's time to address something challenging, preparation matters. Before diving in, take a moment to center yourself and think about how you want to approach the conversation. Lead with curiosity: "I'd like to hear your perspective on this so we can figure out the best path forward together." Tackling tough topics with intentionality not only resolves issues—it builds deeper trust along the way.

Conversations have the power to build bridges that create lasting, meaningful relationships. Imagine what's possible when you approach each interaction with curiosity, empathy, and care. Whether you're navigating sensitive moments, laying groundwork, or having a one-on-one, these everyday exchanges can become opportunities to connect, grow, and build something truly impactful—together.

YOUR CHALLENGE

Make a Seismic Shift in Your Conversations

Pick a conversation to approach with curiosity and intention. Start with an open-ended question like "What's been on your mind lately?" or "How are things really going? *Really?*" Let the conversation flow naturally and focus on listening—not just to their words but to the emotions beneath them. Avoid jumping in to fix or steer the discussion; instead, ask thoughtful follow-ups like "Can you tell me more about that?" or "What's been the most challenging part for you?" Lean into the opportunity to connect on a deeper level. Notice how slowing down and truly listening transforms not just the conversation—but the relationship itself.

SHIFT YOUR LANGUAGE

Does the language you use accelerate connection or erode connection?

YOUR words matter. Choose them wisely.

CHAPTER SIX

SHIFT YOUR LANGUAGE

"Good words are worth much and cost little."

—GEORGE HERBERT

"I know nothing in the world that has as much power as a word."

—EMILY DICKINSON

It was a beautiful, bright morning in La Jolla, California, with waves crashing against the stunning coastline and seals sunbathing on the sand, when I met Marshall in person for the first time. I was there to be vetted for his 100 Coaches group, and I came prepared: new suit, new bag, laptop in hand, ready to put my best foot forward.

What I didn't expect was Marshall's invitation: "Let's go for a walk along the ocean." *A walk?* I had been gearing up for a formal meeting, not a brisk ten-thousand-step stroll. But off we went, me clacking alongside him in my impractical pumps, trying not to limp too visibly as we hit our stride.

As we walked, Marshall asked about my story. I launched into my professional credentials with practiced confidence: "I'm a chaired professor at Loyola University, I run a successful coaching practice, and my first book on connection is about to be published." Then, almost instinctively, I added, "But honestly, I didn't think I'd be divorced and a single mom at this stage in my life."

Marshall stopped midstep, turned to me, and said, "Do you know what you just did?" His words hung in the salty air. "When you said 'but,' you erased everything that came before it. You negated all of your accomplishments by focusing on what you don't have instead of what you do."

Cue the aha moment. How often do we sabotage our own confidence—or diminish someone else's—with a single word? How often do the words we choose shift the entire energy of a conversation, turning connection into critique and curiosity into defensiveness?

Marshall's advice was simple but transformative: Replace "but" with "and." Instead of "I'm doing well professionally, but I'm frustrated personally," say, "I'm doing great professionally, and personally, I'm trying to figure things out." That small tweak changes everything—it acknowledges both the wins and the struggles, creating space for the complexities that life, work, and leadership always hold.

That walk was more than just a vetting for 100 Coaches—it was a master class in the power of language. Marshall's "no buts" approach has become a powerful leadership strategy for me, changing the way I communicate. It's a glimpse into how minor adjustments to our everyday language can reshape our impact and interactions.

The Seismic Shift in Language

Have you ever noticed how certain words shape the way you experience a situation? Small phrases like "just," "should have," or "why didn't you" might seem harmless, yet they shape how you experience situations, how others perceive your words, and even how you feel about your own work. They influence the tone of a conversation, signaling what's valued—and what's not. And more often than not, they reflect something deeper: how you process situations internally.

Think about the tiny word "just."

- *I just need to finish this report.*
- *I just have to get through this meeting.*
- *I just need a few minutes of your time.*

At first glance, "just" seems harmless—maybe even polite. But more often than not, it minimizes. We use it to downplay the significance of our own work, making tasks seem smaller than they are. And when we use it in requests, we unintentionally diminish the importance of what we're asking.

The way you speak to others starts with how you speak to yourself. If you constantly frame your work as just something to check off, you reinforce the idea that the real work—the important work—is always happening somewhere else. If you tell yourself, *I just need to push through* or *I just have to make it to the weekend*, you subtly shift into a survival mindset rather than one of engagement and purpose.

The way you speak to others starts with how you speak to yourself.

And when you use "just" with others—*I just need you to take care of this*—it might seem like a way to soften the ask, to make it feel less demanding. Yet to the other person, it can send the opposite message: *This isn't important, so I'm handing it off to you.*

Start paying attention to your inner language. Notice the words you use, both in your own thoughts and in your conversations. When phrases like "I just," "I can't," "This always happens," or "They'll never get it" come up, pause. How could you say it differently? How might your words create possibilities instead of shutting things down?

Try replacing "just" with a more intentional phrase:

- *This isn't big, however, it's essential.*

- *I need a few minutes of your time for something important.*
- *I have a task I'd love your help with—it matters.*

Because here's the thing—language shapes perception, trust, and confidence. A single word can make a request feel small or significant, turn a challenge into an obligation, or shift a moment of possibility into one of doubt.

I'm not saying you should avoid tough conversations or tiptoe around your words. Honest feedback and clear expectations matter. What I am saying is that the way you phrase things makes a difference—because your words set the tone for connection. They shape how others feel about themselves, their work, and their place on the team.

Language can either build trust or erode it. Over time, small shifts in how you communicate—such as choosing words that empower rather than diminish—can transform how people show up. This is the seismic shift in language: moving from criticism to support. If you want people to feel safe sharing ideas and taking risks, use words that invite engagement.

Language can either build trust or erode it. Over time, small shifts in how you communicate—such as choosing words that empower rather than diminish—can transform how people show up.

Say It Better

When I interviewed Sam Horn for this book, she brought her signature charm, wisdom, and a big black hat—a playful nod to her Texas roots and a memorable choice that embodies her unique communication style. Sam, the author of *Talking on Eggshells*, has a gift for breaking down complex communication challenges into plain, practical shifts that anyone can use.

During our conversation, she emphasized how small, intentional changes in language can make a huge difference in how your words land—and how others respond.

Here are some of the standout takeaways from our conversation.

Turn "Should" into "Next Time"

Sam explained how the word *should* often feels critical, focusing on past mistakes and putting people on the defensive. Instead, she suggests focusing on the desired future behavior.

- Instead of: "You should have brought this up in the meeting."
- Try: "Next time, let's bring this up during the meeting."

This small shift moves the conversation away from blame and toward coaching, opening up space for learning and improvement.

Reframe "No" and "Can't" as "Yes, As Soon As"

Words like "no" or "can't" feel like dead ends, shutting down momentum. Sam suggests keeping the focus on possibilities instead.

- Instead of: "No, we can't start the meeting because not everyone is here."
- Try: "Yes, we can start as soon as everyone arrives."

This shift redirects attention to actionable solutions, keeping conversations forward-focused and productive.

Language shapes perception, trust, and confidence. A simple word can change everything.

Courtesy Instead of Command

A phrase like "You have to" can sound harsh and trigger resistance. Sam recommends softening the tone with respect and collaboration.

- Instead of: "You have to finish this by Friday."
- Try: "If you could get this done by Friday, it would really help the team."

This approach invites cooperation and fosters mutual respect, creating a more positive dynamic.

Turn "There's Nothing I Can Do" into "Let Me See . . ."

When someone hears "There's nothing I can do," it can feel dismissive, cutting off trust. Sam encourages finding ways to show effort and empathy, even when options are limited.

- Instead of: "There's nothing I can do; it's policy."
- Try: "Let me see what I can do to find an alternative."

This subtle shift shows willingness to explore possibilities, building trust even in tough situations.

Sam's advice is a reminder that language can be a bridge. The words we choose can either connect us or create distance. And the best part? These small shifts make a big impact—and you can start using them right away.

Marshall on Shifting Your Language

Michelle shared the story of our first meeting in La Jolla. What Michelle realized during that walk—the unintended impact of a single word—is something I've seen in leaders all over the world. Because it's not just *but*.

Here are four simple word changes you can make to improve connection:

1. “Next time” instead of “Should”
2. “Yes, as soon as” instead of “No”
3. “If you could” instead of “You have to”
4. “Let me see” instead of “There’s nothing I can do”

It's a pattern—a deeply ingrained habit that shows up in three subtle words that can be surprisingly damaging: *no*, *but*, and *however*.

Someone shares an idea, and the first response is, "No, that won't work . . ." or "Yes, but . . ." or "That's true; however . . ."

Said with a smile, these words can feel polite—even helpful. But underneath the surface, they carry a different message: *You're wrong*. Or at the very least, *You're not quite right—and I know better.*

It doesn't matter how well-intentioned your tone is. When you start a sentence with "no," "but," or "however," it puts the other person on the defensive. It shifts the dynamic from collaboration to competition. And for leaders already prone to needing to "win" (see the previous chapter), it turns everyday conversations into battles for control.

Want to test this in real time? Try tracking it. For one week, keep a scorecard. Count how often you or your colleagues start sentences with those three words. The number will surprise you—and the patterns might too.

When I work with clients, I sometimes tally their usage silently during our first session. Then I'll say, "We've been talking for about an hour, and you've used 'no,' 'but,' or 'however' seventeen times."

It's not an accusation. It's a mirror. And that's often where the real coaching begins.

One executive I worked with started keeping a daily tally and even had a colleague charge her a dollar every time she slipped. The dollars added up fast—but so did her awareness. Over time, her conversations shifted. Her team opened up. Trust rose. Resistance dropped. Why? Because she had stopped unintentionally correcting or overriding every idea that wasn't hers.

I once taught this concept in a session with telecom executives. One leader insisted he'd never fall into the trap—and even bet $100 on it. Later that day, during lunch, I asked where he was from.

"Singapore," he said.

"Singapore? That's a great city," I replied.

Without missing a beat, he responded, "Yeah, it's great, but . . ."

He caught himself mid-sentence, laughed, and handed me a hundred bucks.

That's how ingrained the habit is. Even when we know better. Even when we're trying not to do it. Even when it costs us.

Language is never just about words. It's about tone, timing, and intention. So before you jump in with a "no," "but," or "however," pause and ask yourself:

- *Will this comment increase the other person's commitment?*
- *Will this improve my relationship with this person?*

At work, if the answer is no, it might not be worth saying. At home? It's almost *never* worth saying.

So what's the alternative?

Pause before responding. Eliminate qualifiers like *but* and *however*. End your encouragement with a period, not a comma. And instead of jumping to judgment or correction, shift into curiosity. Ask questions that invite others in:

- "Will you tell me more?"
- "How did you come to that?"
- "What do you need from me to move forward?"

These small shifts in language create big shifts in trust, ownership, and collaboration.

How to Build Bridges with Your Language

Shifting your language is about choosing words that foster meaningful connection. Think about the language you use every day—does it create a space where people feel safe to share, or does it unintentionally shut them down? Often, we don't even realize we're doing it. That's why it's so important to pause, reflect, and choose words that open up dialogue.

Here are some changes you can make to help your words land better and encourage others to engage with you.

1 START WITH YOURSELF

How you speak to yourself shapes how you show up for others. Start paying attention to your self-talk—does it lean toward criticism or support? A thought like *How could I mess that up?* can be reframed into *What can I learn from this?* When you treat yourself with kindness, that same understanding naturally extends to those around you.

2 MAKE SOME SMALL SHIFTS

Simple language tweaks can make a huge difference. Swap *get to* for *have to*—you don't *have* to lead a tough conversation; you *get* to build trust. Replace *but* with *and*—you're doing a great job, *and* here's something we can strengthen. Swap *next time* for *should*—not "You should have done this" but "Next time, let's try this." Small words, big impact.

3 FOCUS ON POSSIBILITIES, NOT ROADBLOCKS

When challenges arise, reactive language like "no" or "can't" quickly stall momentum. Instead of saying, "We can't move forward until we have more details," how about saying, "We can move forward as soon as we gather all the necessary details." This shift keeps the conversation focused on solutions and the future. Similarly, using "we" instead of "you" in challenging situations creates a sense of shared responsibility, inviting collaboration rather than blame.

4 REFRAME CRITICISM INTO COACHING

Feedback doesn't have to feel like a critique. Instead of saying, "This should have included more detail," try saying something like, "How can we add more detail to make this stronger?" This language tweak turns feedback into a partnership, helping your team feel empowered rather than judged. It positions you as a coach focused on growth and improvement.

5 LEAD WITH COURTESY, NOT COMMANDS

Sometimes, the smallest shifts make the biggest impact. Commands like "You need to" can feel harsh or authoritarian, but softer phrases like "If you could" or "Would you be able to" show respect and cooperation. This kind of language fosters a culture where people feel valued and appreciated, making it easier to inspire buy-in and collaboration.

These word adjustments might seem minor, but they can completely change how your words land and how others engage with you. By choosing positive language, you'll create a culture where people feel safe, valued, and inspired to share their best ideas.

YOUR CHALLENGE

Make a Seismic Shift in Your Language

Choose one word or phrase to adjust in your everyday conversations. Replace *should* with *next time* to encourage growth, swap *and* for *but* to keep possibilities open, or use *get to* instead of *have to* to reframe tasks with a sense of gratitude. Try these shifts in a meeting, a one-on-one, or even a quick email, and see how they change the tone of your conversations. Small adjustments like these can create meaningful impact.

SHIFT YOUR ENERGY

Does your energy set the tone you want?

YOUR energy is not only contagious, it enters the room before you do.

CHAPTER SEVEN

SHIFT YOUR ENERGY

"Leaders who show up with optimism and confidence create teams that thrive."

—MICHELLE K. JOHNSTON

It was one of those mornings where everything felt like it was falling into place. I was about to give a big presentation at a prestigious law firm. My outfit was on point, and the pièce de résistance? A pair of fabulous heels that screamed confidence.

As I grabbed my bag to head out the door, I caught sight of my pandemic pup, Millie. Her head was tilted, her eyes wide with the quintessential "You forgot to walk me" look. And wouldn't you know—Millie was right. I had forgotten to walk her.

I swapped the flashy heels for a pair of comfortable flats, promising myself it'd just be a quick lap around the block. My pup trotted happily, tail wagging, blissfully unaware of the day's agenda. I finished the walk, rushed back inside, grabbed my bag, and headed straight to the car.

It wasn't until I arrived at the law firm, stepped out of the car, and glanced down that I noticed. My feet. Still in the dog-walking shoes. Those brand-new heels were back home, sitting by the door, completely forgotten.

My old inner perfectionist would have turned critical, saying something like *How could you forget your new shoes? Now you're going on stage in these ugly things?* That kind of negative self-talk would have followed me right into the room, affecting the mood of the entire audience.

But this time, I didn't let it happen.

Instead, I took a deep breath, chuckled, and thought, *These shoes are ugly, but does it really matter?* I knew I couldn't turn back, so I decided to let it go.

When I walked into the law firm's beautiful offices, I brought positive, confident energy—not because my outfit was flawless but because my mindset was.

During the presentation, I even shared the story.

"Look, I left my amazing heels by the door today," I confessed, gesturing to the flats and sharing about my quick walk with the pup. "But here's the thing: Did anyone die? No. Is my ability to connect with you all diminished because of these frumpy flats? Absolutely not."

The room burst into laughter, and we carried that lightness and connection through the rest of the session.

The truth is, *how* I showed up mattered far more than what was on my feet. Instead of giving in to negative self-talk, I chose to bring an *"It's all going to be fine"* energy—because energy is contagious. Whether you're leading a team, presenting on stage, or simply walking into a room, the tone you set is palpable. People feed off the energy you bring, and your presence speaks before you even say a word. Your energy enters the scene before you do.

People feed off the energy you bring, and your presence speaks before you even say a word. Your energy enters the scene before you do.

This moment was a perfect illustration of something Marshall has been coaching me on for years. His mantra? "Let it go."

It's a reminder to stop clinging to the small stuff—the frustrations, the self-doubt, the need to control every detail—and instead focus on showing up fully in the moment. Because let's be real—you can't bring inspiring energy when you're stuck in your own head, replaying mistakes, fixating on what didn't go right, or worrying about things no one else even notices.

Mel Robbins takes this even further in her *New York Times* best-selling book, *The Let Them Theory*. She explains that much of our anxiety comes from trying to control people and situations that aren't ours to manage. Her approach? Two simple steps:

1. Let Them, then
2. Let Me.

> **LET THEM:** Let people do what they're going to do. Stop wasting energy trying to fix, convince, or control. Release the frustration of wanting others to behave a certain way.
>
> **LET ME:** Shift your focus inward. Decide how you want to show up, regardless of the chaos around you. Instead of letting external factors dictate your energy, take ownership of it.

When Mel embraced this mindset, it changed everything—her personal life, her professional life, her entire approach to relationships. And that's the real shift: Your energy is a choice.

You set the tone for every room you walk into.

The question is—what kind of energy are you bringing?

The Seismic Shift in Energy

When I first mapped out this book, I thought I'd include a chapter on shifting your environment—how the spaces where we work affect how people interact. I was ready to dive into how your Zoom backdrop should reflect your personality and your brand. And while those things matter, the more I spoke with different leaders, the more they brought it back to one core idea: The real environment that affects leadership isn't the physical one around you—it's the one inside you.

The real environment that affects leadership isn't the physical one around you—it's the one inside you.

And the more I thought about it, the more it made total sense.

Sure, a great physical environment can help. But if your internal environment is filled with stress, doubt, or negativity, it doesn't matter how beautiful your office is—people will feel it. And on the flip side? A leader who brings clarity, confidence, and calm can transform even the most chaotic space.

Your energy carries more weight than your physical surroundings. And hear this loud and clear: Personality doesn't define it—choice does.

You've probably heard the phrase, "Your attitude determines your altitude." And sure, positive energy matters. But let's be real—leaders are human. No one wakes up every single day feeling super positive, upbeat, and ready to take on the world.

That's why this shift isn't about pretending—it's about being intentional with the energy you bring. Some days, you'll walk into a meeting feeling great, ready to inspire. Other days, challenges will hit, and you won't have the same spark. That's okay. What matters is how you *choose* to show up.

That doesn't mean slapping on a fake smile when you're struggling. It means acknowledging where you are, being honest about it, and still leading with steadiness and optimism. Instead of suppressing a bad day, own it. Instead of aiming for perfection, let people see you as a full human. People don't need perfect leaders—they need real ones.

We've all seen how one toxic person can derail an entire group. It's the classic bad apple effect—negativity spreads like wildfire, stalling momentum and creating tension. And when that bad apple is the leader? The damage is immediate. Stress ripples through the team, engagement drops, trust erodes, and the best people either burn out or leave.

And here's the thing: Just as negativity spreads, so does positivity.

A leader who brings positive clarity and a grounded presence can completely change the atmosphere. That energy sparks focus, confidence, and connection. It creates a space where trust grows, people feel motivated, and challenges become opportunities instead of obstacles.

When I think of someone who embodies this kind of energy, I think of Hoda Kotb. I watched Hoda on the *The Today Show* for years just to see her infectious energy. Her laugh and spirit elevated the interactions and interviews she participated in. Her goodness was palpable, even through the television. And now I'm following her in her new venture, JOY101. To me, Hoda embodies intentional, positive, and genuine energy.

This is the seismic shift: recognizing that your energy is something you choose. Not fake, not forced—*real*. And when you choose to lead with energy that's honest, intentional, and empowering, it's an absolute game changer.

The Three-Step Process for Shifting Your Energy

So how do you make that shift—especially on the days when you feel drained, distracted, or just not at your best?

That's something my friend and colleague Morag Barrett thinks about a lot.

I first met Morag at a 100 Coaches gathering in New York City in 2021, where we convened together as a group to watch many of our colleagues receive awards at the virtual Thinkers50 awards ceremony. We hit it off immediately, and I quickly learned that in addition to being an executive coach and the CEO of SkyeTeam, Morag also ran leadership academies.

Years later, when a leader from the New Orleans Saints and Pelicans came to me—holding my first book—and asked if I could run a Seismic Shift Leadership Academy for their leaders, Morag was the first person I called.

When you show up with energy that is clear, intentional, and human, it invites others to do the same.

The two of us speak the same language: Leadership is about connection. We both believe that cultures of connection drive results. That shared belief led us to colead what is now the Benson Leadership Academy, serving the New Orleans Saints, Pelicans, Benson Automotive Group, Corporate Realty, and Benson Capital Partners.

In our work, Morag shared a practical framework that she first introduced in her book *You, Me, We*. She calls it "Look Up, Show Up, Step Up." It's a quick way to reset your energy in real time—and it starts from within.

1 LOOK UP: HOW DO I FEEL?

Before you engage with others, check in with yourself. What energy are you bringing? Are you feeling clear and engaged—or scattered and reactive? Maybe you're somewhere in the middle. That's okay. The goal isn't to force a mood shift—it's to get honest about where you are.

Try this: Ask yourself, *If I had to evaluate my energy right now on a scale from one to ten, where would I be?* For instance, a one might mean you're running on empty, distracted, or completely overwhelmed. And a ten might mean you're feeling calm, focused, and fully ready to take on any challenge.

Even if your number isn't as high as you'd like, pause and focus on what *is* working. If you're at a six, ask yourself: *Why am I not a five?* Maybe it's the great conversation you had this morning. Maybe it's the coffee that hit just right. Acknowledging what's good—even when things aren't *great*—can anchor your energy in something positive.

2 SHOW UP: HOW DO I WANT OTHERS TO FEEL IN MY PRESENCE?

Once you know where you are, the next question is: *How do I want others to feel?*

Whether it's a one-on-one conversation, a Zoom meeting, or a team huddle, your energy sets the tone. Are you bringing calm, confidence, and focus—or stress, frustration, and overwhelm?

And here's the thing: Even if you're not at 100 percent, you can still be intentional about the energy you bring.

Let's say you had a tough morning and you're feeling drained. You don't have to fake enthusiasm. You can honestly say, "Hey, team, it's been a long morning, and I'm here. Let's work through this together." That kind of grounded honesty builds trust.

3 **STEP UP: WHAT AM I GOING TO DO?**

This is where action happens—where you get to be intentional and choose how to show up at your best. Ask yourself: *What's one small shift I can make right now to bring better energy into the room?*

Maybe it's as simple as taking a deep breath before a meeting to try to ground yourself and get present. Maybe it's pausing before reacting in the moment—choosing to ask a question instead of jumping to conclusions. Maybe it's acknowledging your state and asking for support—modeling that it's okay to not always be at 100 percent.

And here's the real magic: When you show up with energy that is clear, intentional, and human, it invites others to do the same.

Your Energy—Your Choice

I see this level of energy ownership with one of my coaching clients, Sahil, the CEO of multiple urgent care facilities in California. During a meeting with his executive team, Sahil looked each person in the eye and said with quiet authority, "Own your energy."

He reminded them that the energy they bring has a massive impact on their teams, their patients, and the broader community. "You control your energy. No excuses."

Sahil doesn't just say this to others. He lives it himself. He leads three centers in a community deeply rooted in family and tradition. Every single day, he brings a steady, grounded presence—no matter what's happening around him. His team trusts him because they know what to expect from him: He brings clarity, optimism, and steadiness to every interaction.

One of his team members even developed a practice around this idea. Before stepping into any patient's room, she taps twice on the door. It's her way of resetting—of letting go of whatever came before and choosing to bring her best energy to that moment.

Hearing that piece of advice reminded me of a story Alan Mulally once shared with me. Alan, the legendary former CEO of Boeing and Ford, said that during his time at Ford, he realized that as the "turnaround guy," all eyes were on him during a pivotal point in the company's story—employees, shareholders, the media, the public. If Ford was going to regain trust, Alan had to embody it first. He wasn't just leading the company; he *was* the company, at least in the public's eyes. And he understood that his successful experiences and positive energy, presence, and attitude would set the tone for everyone else.

If he walked out of Ford's headquarters looking defeated, the stock prices would drop. If he looked stressed, employees would panic and momentum would stall. He realized that something as small as how he carried himself walking in and out of the building had an impact.

So he made a deliberate choice: No matter how turbulent things were, he would walk in and out of the headquarters with a calm, steady smile. But make no mistake—this wasn't about faking it. Alan's confidence wasn't blind optimism; it was grounded in strategy, preparation, and an unshakable belief in his team's ability to execute. That smile wasn't a mask—it was a reflection of his conviction that Ford would turn things around. And they did.

Energy First—Environment Second

Remember Garry Ridge all the way back from chapter one? The "consciously incompetent, probably wrong, and roughly right" chairman and CEO of WD-40 Company? When I sat down with him to talk about his leadership journey, I wanted to hear about the incredible office transformation he'd led—the way he intentionally designed the space to foster deeper connection.

But it quickly became clear that long before the new office was built, the energy was already there.

Their old building? It was bad. Like, *really* bad. Built in the 1970s, the office had low ceilings, dark spaces, outdated everything. It was the kind of place you walk into and immediately feel the weight of fluorescent lighting and beige cubicles. The kind of space that, on the surface, shouldn't inspire anything other than a countdown to the end of the workday.

And yet, when Garry asked his employees why they stayed, why they thrived even in that less-than-inspiring space, the answer was straightforward: "Because we loved being here."

Not because of the layout. Not because of the high-end amenities. Because of the energy—the way people showed up.

You can imagine the kind of energy Garry brought to his team, right? The kind that says, *I see you. I respect you. I value what you bring to the table. I trust you to be human.* He wasn't nitpicking flaws or micromanaging tasks—he was catching people doing something right. Asking questions. Showing up with curiosity and humility. He was building an environment where people felt seen, heard, valued, appreciated, and respected.

And none of that required a state-of-the-art office. When a space is filled with honesty, levity, and optimism, that's what people respond to.

Because connection starts with how you show up. When you walk into the room engaged, present, and fully human, that energy fills the space—whether you're in a drab office or a sleek new headquarters. People feel it. They respond to it. They mirror it.

Connection starts with how you show up. When you walk into the room engaged, present, and fully human, that energy fills the space—whether you're in a drab office or a sleek new headquarters.

And when you don't? They feel that too. No matter how beautiful your surroundings are.

Does that mean environment is irrelevant? No. The spaces where we work and lead do impact our energy—just not in the way most people think.

When Garry finally had the opportunity to design WD-40's new headquarters, he didn't just create a modern office. He built a space that reinforced the kind of energy that was already alive in his team.

- Every office—including his—was the same size. No oversized executive suites. No unspoken hierarchy.
- No assigned parking spaces—because leadership isn't about status.
- Open spaces designed for "collision zones"—areas where people would naturally cross paths, strike up conversations, and connect.
- A cantina, not a cafeteria—a space meant for gathering, not just eating.
- Meeting rooms named after cities where other WD-40 employees worked so when they visited, they saw themselves reflected in the space.

Every detail was deliberately geared toward creating an environment that amplified the energy of the people inside it. And when they finally moved in? The energy they had already built expanded into the space.

Sprinkle in a Little Gratitude

One of the easiest—and most surprisingly powerful—ways to shift your energy is through gratitude.

Let me introduce you to the phenom known as Chester Elton.

Chester is a *New York Times* best-selling author who's been called the Apostle of Appreciation, the Dalai Lama of Workplace Trauma, and the Minister of Motivation. (I know. Quite the resume.) I've had the joy of learning from him over the years, and one of the things I admire most is how he makes gratitude feel doable—something you can reach for anytime, anywhere, even in the middle of a chaotic day.

After decades of studying what makes great leaders, Chester landed on something surprisingly simple: The most effective ones lead with gratitude.

After decades of studying what makes great leaders, Chester landed on something surprisingly simple: The most effective ones lead with gratitude.

Not in a big, flashy, performative way. Not through awards or speeches. But in quiet, consistent moments of noticing. Of naming what's working. Of pausing long enough to really see the people—and let them know they matter.

If you're anything like me, you might hear "practice gratitude" and think, *Okay, but how?* Chester will tell you that it starts with being specific. Instead of a vague "Great job," you might say, "Thanks for how you led that meeting—it helped the team stay focused and energized." Specificity makes a huge difference. The more precise the appreciation, the more it lands.

And then there's the personal side. Some people feel seen when you acknowledge them publicly; others appreciate a quiet, thoughtful note or a few words after a meeting. You don't have to get it perfect—you just get to be thoughtful. Start to notice how people respond and adjust as you go.

Timing helps too. Chester always reminds leaders not to save their appreciation for special occasions. Say it now. Let it be natural, a part of your regular rhythm. And when you can, connect it to something meaningful—help someone see how what they did contributes to the bigger picture, to a shared value, or to the mission you're all working toward.

Little by little, that practice becomes part of how you lead. Maybe you start a meeting by naming something that's going well. Maybe you close out a Friday with a quick thank-you message or two. Whatever it looks like for you, it doesn't need to be grand. It just needs to be genuine.

And here's where it loops back to energy. When you slow down to appreciate what's good—even in a stressful moment—something shifts. Your nervous system settles. Your outlook clears. You feel a little more grounded, a little more connected, a little more you.

Marshall on Shifting Your Energy

Michelle is absolutely right—the energy you bring as a leader can make or break your culture.

One of the most extraordinary examples I've seen is Frances Hesselbein. Frances led the Girl Scouts of the USA for fourteen years, transforming it into one of America's most admired nonprofits. But what made Frances unforgettable wasn't just what she accomplished—it was how she treated people.

I'll never forget the time she invited me to speak to a group of regional Girl Scout CEOs. These were some of the most respected leaders in the organization, and I was honored to be there. The only problem? My schedule was packed, and the only day I could do it was a Saturday.

When I apologized, Frances didn't hesitate. "You work Saturday; we work Saturday. You're the volunteer, not us."

Problem solved. Except—I had another one.

"Frances . . . I'm out of clean clothes. I've been traveling nonstop and need to do laundry before the session. Is there any way you can help?"

She didn't miss a beat. "Of course. We have laundry facilities at the Edith Macy Center. Just leave your clothes in a pile—we'll take care of the rest."

I did what she said. Dropped my sweaty socks and underwear in a heap and went off to prepare my talk.

The next morning, I sat down to breakfast with the regional CEOs, coffee in hand—and saw Frances walking down the hallway.

Carrying my laundry.

I was mortified.

This was a woman with twenty-three honorary PhDs. A Presidential Medal of Freedom. A legacy of national leadership. And there she was—walking past senior executives—with my laundry in her arms.

She didn't say a word. She didn't need to.

Her energy said it all.

That's what leadership looks like.

No hierarchy. No fanfare. Just service. Presence. Humility. And everyone saw it.

Frances didn't just talk about the importance of showing up as a positive, humble leader—she lived it. And in that one quiet gesture, she taught me more than most leaders could in a lifetime.

That's what shifting your energy looks like.

Another favorite example comes from a member of our 100 Coaches community, Telly Leung. Telly played the title role of *Aladdin* on Broadway more than one thousand times—one thousand nights of singing the same songs, saying the same lines, wearing the same costume.

I once asked him, "How do you do it? How do you bring the energy night after night?"

Telly shared that when he was eight years old, he saw his first Broadway show. It was magical. The voices, the music, the energy—it moved him in a way nothing else ever had.

He told me, "Every night I go out on that stage, I think of that little boy. And I say, 'This one's for you.'"

It didn't matter if it was his first performance or his thousandth. For someone in the audience, it was their first time, and that made it matter.

The most powerful message you send as a leader doesn't come from what you say—it comes from how you show up.

- *When things go wrong, do you bring panic—or presence?*
- *When someone shares a hard truth, do you shut it down—or applaud the honesty?*
- *When someone needs help, do you delegate—or roll up your sleeves?*

Your energy is a choice.

Like Telly stepping onto the stage for his thousandth performance, remind yourself before you step into any room or even conversation: *It's showtime.*

Not as a performance but as a commitment—to show up fully, bring intentional energy, and offer the presence others need.

How to Shift Your Energy

Your energy is your responsibility. It's not dictated by your circumstances, your to-do list, or the mood of the people around you. It's something you choose—moment by moment, interaction by interaction. It's something you own.

Ready to take ownership of your energy? Here's where to start.

1 LET IT GO (FOR REAL THIS TIME)

Not everything deserves your energy. Yet how often do you let a tech glitch, a late email, or an offhand comment pull you into a spiral? Mel Robbins's "let them, let me" theory is the perfect reset. *Let them*—let people do what they do. *Let me*—choose how you respond. Instead of asking, *Why did this happen?* try *What's my next best move?* Because your energy isn't controlled by what happens—it's controlled by you.

2 DECIDE HOW YOU WANT TO SHOW UP

Your energy isn't about always being upbeat—it's about being intentional. Before your next meeting, conversation, or decision, pause. *How do I want people to feel when they engage with me?* Like Frances, lead with humility. Like Telly, bring fresh heart and presence. The energy you bring is *your* choice.

3 CREATE THE RIGHT ENVIRONMENT

Your energy starts from within, but your surroundings play a role too. If you want a connected, energized team, think about the spaces where they spend their time. Could you create places for spontaneous connection—"collision zones" where people naturally cross paths? Maybe turn the break room into a *real* recharge space. A gratitude board where people can highlight wins, big or small. Even small rituals—playing music, hosting a community service day, or having a lighthearted team tradition—can shift the atmosphere. Set the stage for the kind of energy you want to cultivate.

4 MAKE GRATITUDE YOUR BASELINE

Gratitude shifts your energy—and the energy of everyone around you. You don't have to wait for a big win to name what's working. Small efforts count. Be specific. Say thank you. Let people know how they're adding value. When you do, you create a space where people feel seen and show up at their best.

Bringing intentional energy isn't about being always "on" or relentlessly positive. It's about showing up with purpose. The way you walk into a room, the energy you bring to conversations, the presence you bring to challenges—it all matters. You don't have to wait for the perfect conditions. You can start shaping your energy right now.

YOUR CHALLENGE

Make a Seismic Shift in Your Energy

Pick one situation—maybe it's a meeting, a one-on-one conversation, or even a quick check-in with your team. Before you step in, pause and ask yourself: *How do I want to show up in this moment?* Maybe that means bringing calm instead of letting stress take over. Maybe it means choosing curiosity over jumping to conclusions. Or maybe it just means being honest. If you're having a hard day, you can say, "I'm a little off today, but I'm here. Let's figure this out together." Because the kind of energy that builds trust and connection comes from presence. When you show up as your full, human self, you make space for others to do the same.

CONCLUSION

For a long time, I thought my second book would be about transforming workplace culture—about how to create environments where people feel truly connected, valued, and engaged.

And that's true. Workplaces *do* need to change. We've seen what happens when people feel disconnected: burnout, disengagement, leaders struggling to get through to their teams. Something has to shift.

And at first, I thought the answer was a *culture* shift. But the more I worked with leaders, the more I realized: You can't change culture without first changing the way you show up. Because here's the truth—culture isn't a policy or a program. It's not a set of company values framed on the wall or a new initiative handed down from leadership.

Culture is the lived experience of how people interact, engage, and connect. It's how people feel when they walk into a room, how they experience their meetings, how they show up for conversations. It's the energy of a place, the way people communicate, the trust (or lack thereof) that shapes every interaction.

I had been thinking about connection on a large scale—how to get entire organizations to embrace it. But what I kept coming back to was this: Connection isn't something you implement from the top down. It's not a corporate strategy. It's not a checklist. It's not something you delegate.

Connection starts with YOU.

And if you take one thing away from this book, let it be that.

As a leader, how you show up sets the tone for everything.

Your energy. Your presence. Your words. Your actions.

The way you enter a room. The way you hold space for a conversation. The way you handle stress, conflict, and uncertainty.

It all ripples outward.

Your team will never be more connected than YOU are.

If you're disengaged, they will be too. If you're overwhelmed and reactive, they will mirror that. If you hold people at arm's length, they won't lean in.

You can't expect your people to engage deeply if you're running on empty. You can't foster trust if you're too distracted to be present. You can't create meaningful relationships if you're prioritizing speed over connection, efficiency over humanity.

So instead of writing a book about shifting the way workplaces function, I wrote a book about shifting the way YOU function. Because when connection isn't just something you talk about but something you *live*—when it's embedded in your presence, your schedule, your daily choices—*everything else follows*.

Prioritize Connection, and the Results will Follow

If you've made it this far, I hope you've already felt something shift within you—maybe a realization, a moment of clarity, or even just the spark of a new way to approach your leadership. That's the goal of this book.

Because this is so much more than a collection of strategies to lead more effectively. This is about leading in a way that feels more fulfilling and more aligned with who you truly are.

Each of these shifts stands on its own, yet together, they create a powerful picture of what it looks like to lead with clarity, connection, and intention. Some will feel like second nature to you. Others might stretch you in ways you didn't expect. But every single one is essential.

1 ## SHIFT YOUR PERSPECTIVE

To focus on *connection*. Because the only way you're going to succeed is through your ability to connect with others.

2 ## SHIFT YOUR PRIORITIES

To focus on *what fuels you*. Because you can't give your best to others if you're running on empty.

3 ## SHIFT YOUR CALENDAR

To focus on *your most important relationships*. Because what you give your time to reveals what (and who) matters most.

4 ## SHIFT YOUR MEETINGS

To focus on *engagement*. Because people feel seen, heard, valued, respected, and appreciated when they are a part of the problem-solving and decision-making processes.

5 ## SHIFT YOUR CONVERSATIONS

To focus on dialogue. Because connection grows when you inquire more—with great questions—and talk less.

6 ## SHIFT YOUR LANGUAGE

To focus on *positivity and possibility*. Because the words you choose shape the reality you're creating every day.

7 ## SHIFT YOUR ENERGY

To focus on *intentionality*. Because the energy you bring sets the tone for everyone around you.

Sometimes, one shift is all it takes. Maybe it's shifting your calendar—finally aligning your time with what actually matters. Maybe it's shifting your energy—recognizing how your presence affects the people around you. Maybe it's shifting your meetings—turning a weekly obligation into a meaningful moment of connection.

For some, maybe it's the sum of all these shifts.

Regardless of where you start, here's what I know: Connection is a gift that drives results and makes everyone happier along the way.

Go Slow to Go Fast

By now, you've probably noticed that these shifts require something unexpected: slowing down. They invite you to pause. To be intentional. To think things through on the front end instead of just reacting in the moment and plowing forward. They call for noticing—your energy, your conversations, your habits, the way you show up.

And maybe that feels like a luxury you don't have. Maybe you're already stretched thin, managing competing priorities, deadlines, and expectations. Maybe the idea of adding anything that isn't directly tied to results feels impossible.

I get it.

Most leaders—myself included—have been conditioned to believe that speed is the goal. Results. Efficiency. Bottom-line performance. We're trained to focus on moving quickly, making decisions, and pushing toward outcomes. But what I've learned—through coaching, research, and my own lived experience—is that the leaders who actually achieve those outcomes get there because they invest in connection first.

And that investment? It's not a distraction. It's not a detour from the "real work." It's what makes the real work *possible*. It's what holds everything else together.

These shifts empower you to lead with more intention, to weave connection into the way you show up every day—into your perspective, your priorities, your calendar, your meetings, your conversations, your language, and your energy. When connection drives your leadership, you deepen trust, you strengthen communication, you unite your teams, and ultimately—results will follow.

So if you're still thinking, *I don't have time for this touchy-feely stuff*, I'd argue that you don't have time *not* to do it. Because the more you neglect connection, the harder everything else becomes. You waste time revisiting the same conversations, managing disengagement, hiring new employees, and putting out fires that could have been prevented in the first place. But when you invest in connection first? You create a foundation where people are aligned, energized, and ready to move—fast.

Leadership Is Within Your Control

We started this journey by looking at a problem so many leaders feel but struggle to name—the kind of disconnection that creeps into teams, meetings, and conversations.

Maybe you've felt it too.

That moment when you look around and realize people are showing up, but they're not fully engaged. The energy in the room isn't bad, exactly, but it isn't great either. And no matter how many strategies you try, something still feels . . . off.

We traced that feeling back to its source—not a broken system, not a lack of effort, but something deeper. The disconnection we feel in our teams, our work, and our lives doesn't start *out there*.

It starts within.

That realization can feel overwhelming. But it's also freeing. Because if disconnection starts with us, then so does the solution.

One of the biggest misconceptions about leadership is that so much of it is out of our control. But here's what I want you to take with you: You have more control than you think.

- If you're running on empty, your team will feel it.
- If you're disengaged, your meetings will be uninspired.
- If you're constantly reacting instead of leading with intention, everything will feel harder than it needs to be.

But the opposite is also true.

- If you bring energy and presence to a conversation, people will mirror it.
- If you create space for real dialogue, engagement will follow.
- If you model connection, trust, and intentionality in the way you lead, it will ripple outward.

That's why these seven shifts help create the foundation of leading in a way that is both effective *and* fulfilling. They're what allow you to create an environment where people—including you—can thrive.

Because, at the end of the day, leadership isn't just about getting things done. It's about the people who make it happen. It's not just about achieving results. It's about how you get there. It's not just about moving fast. It's about making the time to lead with connection.

And that's something you have the power to shift—starting right now.

So take a breath. Let it settle in.

- What's resonating with you?
- Which shift is calling for your attention?

Wherever that pull is, that's where you begin.

One of the best examples of this I've ever seen? My dad.

At the launch party in 2022 for *The Seismic Shift in Leadership*, I stood at the front of the room, sharing stories of remarkable leaders I'd interviewed and learned from. Leaders who didn't just manage people—but listened deeply, showed compassion, inspired trust, and built environments where teams thrived.

As I spoke, I kept glancing at my dad, who was seated in the audience. He was smiling at me, his expression steady and warm, and I suddenly realized that everything I was describing, everything I had learned about connection-driven leadership—he had been modeling all along.

Think back for a moment. Who's the person in your life who embodies the characteristics you admire most? Is it someone who's made you feel seen, heard, and valued?

My dad spent decades at General Motors, moving from market to market every few years. Yet no matter where he went, his reputation preceded him. Even now, years into his retirement, he still receives letters and messages from former employees—notes filled with words like, "You were the most positive leader I've ever worked with" or "You were the best boss I ever had."

He didn't achieve that by chance. He created a space where people wanted to do their best by choosing, every day, to show up in a way that brought people together. He listened, supported, and inspired those around him. And that intentional focus on connection shaped everything.

Fast-forward a few months. It was the day after Thanksgiving, and for the first time in years, it was just me and my dad. With my mom gone and my brother off with his wife and children, the holiday was quieter than usual—just the two of us. The day felt unhurried, the autumn air crisp, and the trees a stunning blend of reds and yellows. We decided to take a walk along the lake near his home, the kind of walk with no agenda, no clock to watch.

As we strolled, I noticed how every so often we'd stop so my dad could chat with someone he knew. Normally, I might have been the one nudging him along—*Dad, we need to keep moving*—but this time, I let it unfold naturally. I watched as he engaged each person he met with a twinkle in his eyes, an elevated energy, and his wonderfully contagious laugh—making each person feel like they were the most important person in the world.

I wonder—have you ever had a moment like that, where you finally slowed down enough to see someone's true character shine through?

That day, I saw my father fully in his element. It was a window into his lifelong practice of leading through connection. He wasn't a boss giving orders or someone focused on outcomes. He was simply showing up for others, listening deeply, and creating a beautiful sense of community. That's who he was—who he still is.

Now, before you start thinking my dad had some kind of perfect life, let me set the record straight. He grew up in poverty in Washington, D.C., raised by a single mother and an alcoholic father. He's told me stories of breaking up furniture for firewood just to stay warm. Life was hard, and the odds weren't in his favor. But he made a choice—a choice to be positive, to persevere, to bring out the best in others. That wasn't luck. It wasn't circumstance. It was a deliberate decision.

What I hope you'll take away is this: Leading through connection starts within. It's not about having the perfect conditions, the perfect team, or the perfect background. It's about deciding how you'll show up—every day, in every situation, in every moment and conversation.

So ask yourself: What's one small way you can be more intentional about how you show up today?

When you choose to engage, inspire, and truly see the people around you, you're creating a ripple effect that changes everything. That choice—to lead with connection—is what transforms not just your leadership but the experience of everyone you lead. It's what makes the work more meaningful, the results more fulfilling, and the relationships more authentic. And it's a choice YOU can start making right now.

ACKNOWLEDGMENTS

Michelle

To Marshall for believing in me, partnering with me, and supporting me in my mission to help others build beautiful connections in their lives.

To my family who are full of loving support: Biz, Dad, Chris, Pat, Steven, Addie, Sydney, Cole, Kevin, Deb, Dave.

To my childhood friends who encouraged me to truly, completely be myself: Kimmy, Laura, Lisa, Kerry, Janet, Jeanette, Kim, Bonnie, Meredith, Heidi, Jim, Kif, Gabe, Heidi, Betty.

To my coffee group, The Betrothed, who are my life advisors: Allison, Anne, Courtney, Dodie, Jeanne, Jennifer, Kendall, Michele.

To my New Orleans compatriots who celebrate the rhythms and rituals of life with me in this amazing city: Kate, Taylor, Ann, Susan, Tasha, Jackie, Suzette, Pam, Ashley, Molly, Kristin, Sara, Cathryn, Sarah, Madhavi, Allison, Jenny, Larry, Tim W.

To Whitney and Blake at New Bridge Studios for helping me capture great content on my podcast that led to many chapters in this book.

To Emilie, the best writing coach and project manager I could ever have asked for.

To Mark for writing the beautiful foreword to the book.

To my clients and colleagues who teach me every single day about connection: Pete, Eden, Amy, Fernis, Chuck, Chris, Brad, Raghu, Katie, Laura, Greg H., Doug, Linley, Greg B., Greg R., Dennis, David, Kendra, Valerie, Bobby, Adam, John, Brit, Bart, Taylor, Amy, Allie.

To my 100 Coaches colleagues who have elevated me to new levels: Morag, Ruth, Jacquelyn, Michael, Scott, Bill, Julie, Sally, Mary, Connie, Linda, Lisa, Dean, Todd, Tricia, Janice, Tammy, Jennifer.

To the leaders highlighted in this book who are role models in connection: Garry, Pete, Bart, Sam, Taylor, Alisa, Chester, Morag, Steven, Sam, Hoda, Mel.

To my incredible team at Amplify Publishing. Naren and Lauren: You were dreams to work with!

Marshall

First, I honor my mentors—Peter Drucker, Frances Hesselbein, Warren Bennis, Ken Blanchard, Paul Hersey, and Alan Mulally—each of whom left a profound mark on my career and leadership philosophy. Their wisdom, generosity, and example have shaped not only my work, but the way I aspire to show up in the world every day.

I am also deeply grateful for the extraordinary 100 Coaches community—a network built on generosity, collaboration, and shared learning. This remarkable group lives the very principles of servant leadership, and I am proud to walk alongside such purpose-driven individuals who lift others with intention and care.

To my family and friends, thank you for your constant support, patience, and encouragement. Your love has been the steady foundation beneath every chapter of this journey, and I carry deep gratitude for your presence in my life.

To my clients and readers around the world—thank you for your trust in my work and for your commitment to becoming not only better leaders, but better colleagues, partners, and human beings. Your growth and impact are the most meaningful legacy of the ideas I've been privileged to share.

Finally, I want to express my deep gratitude to my coauthor, Michelle Johnston. Working alongside you has been both energizing and rewarding. You bring a rare blend of intellect, empathy, and clarity that elevates every conversation and strengthens every idea. I am grateful for the generosity you show in sharing your expertise, and I look forward to seeing the continued impact of your important work on leaders everywhere.

ABOUT THE AUTHORS

Named a Woman of the Year, a Top Ten Executive Coach, and a Top 500 Business Leader, **DR. MICHELLE K. JOHNSTON** is redefining what leadership looks like in today's world. Her bestselling book, *The Seismic Shift in Leadership: How to Thrive in a New Era of Connection*, featured by *Forbes* four times, spotlights real-world leaders who have embraced this shift and are seeing stronger teams and better results because of it.

An award-winning leadership expert and the Clifton A. Morvant Distinguished Professor of Business at Loyola University New Orleans, Michelle teaches leadership and strategic communication with a connection-first lens. She holds a PhD in Communication from Louisiana State University and brings decades of insight to her coaching and keynotes.

She also hosts *The Seismic Shift* podcast, ranked in the Top 10% of all podcasts globally, where she continues the conversation with executives and thought leaders committed to building cultures of connection.

ABOUT THE AUTHORS

MARSHALL GOLDSMITH is the founder of the Marshall Goldsmith Group and 100 Coaches. The inaugural winner of the Lifetime Achievement Award by the Institute of Coaching at Harvard Medical School and a Thinkers50 Management Hall of Fame inductee, he is also a professor of management at the Dartmouth Tuck School of Business and a board member for the Peter Drucker Foundation. He received his PhD from the UCLA Anderson School of Management. In his coaching practice, he has advised more than 200 major CEOs and their management teams. Marshall is the author or editor of more than thirty-five books, including *What Got You Here Won't Get You There*. His most recent book, written with Mark Reiter, is *The Earned Life: Lose Regret, Choose Fulfillment*.